THE JACOBITE REBELLIONS

Text by
MICHAEL BARTHORP
Colour plates by
G A EMBLETON

First published in Great Britain in 1982 by
Osprey Publishing, Elms Court, Chapel Way, Botley,
Oxford OX2 9LP, United Kingdom.
Email: info@ospreypublishing.com

© 1982 Osprey Publishing Ltd.
00 01 02 03 04 10 9 8 7 6 5 4 3 2 1
Also Published as Men-a-Arms 118 *The Jacobite
Rebellions 1689-1745*

ISBN 1 84176 167 2

Back cover Cartography by The Map Studio

Tourist Information by Martin Marix Evans

Filmset in Great Britain
Printed in China through World Print Ltd.

Acknowledgements
The author is grateful, first, for the assistance given in
various ways by Mr W. G. F. Boag of the Scottish
United Services Museum, Miss Sheila Gill of the
Scottish National Portrait Gallery, Mr G. A. Gordon
and Mr R. J. Marrion; second, for permission to
reproduce paintings from their private collections by
the Duke of Atholl, the Earl of Seafield, Miss Fiona
Fraser and Mr Mark Murray Threipland; and third
to the staffs of the Royal Collection, the National
Army Museum and the National Galleries of
Scotland.

FOR A CATALOGUE OF ALL BOOKS PUBLISHED BY
OSPREY MILITARY, AUTOMOTIVE AND AVIATION
PLEASE WRITE TO:

The Marketing Manager, Osprey Direct UK,
PO Box 140, Wellingborough, Northants, NN8 4ZA,
United Kingdom.
Email: info@ospreydirect.co.uk

The Marketing Manager, Osprey Direct USA,
PO Box 130, Sterling Heights, MI 48311-0130, USA.
Email: info@ospreydirectusa.com

VISIT OSPREY AT
www.ospreypublishing.com

FRONT COVER: Jacobite Weapons © Trustees of
the National Museums of Scotland 2000

Chronology of the Jacobite Rebellions

Background

1644   In the Civil War Montrose raises the Highland clans for Charles I against Parliament's allies, the Scottish Covenanters led by the Marquis of Argyll.

1648   Scots change sides but are defeated at Preston by Cromwell.

1650–60   Cromwellian troops under Monk pacify Scotland after defeating Charles II's Scottish army at Dunbar and Worcester.

1660–85   Reign of Charles II. Protestant fears of Roman Catholic succession by James, Duke of York, Charles's brother.

1677   James's daughter, Mary, marries William, Prince of Orange, chief Protestant opponent of Louis XIV of France.

1685   Succession of James II of England and VII of Scotland. Persecution of Covenanters in Scotland. Defeat of Protestant insurrections led by Earl of Argyll in Scotland and Duke of Monmouth in England. James's attempts to restore absolute monarchy, his advancement of Catholics and his garrisoning of Irish Catholic troops in England all increase Protestant hostility to his rule. Birth of a male heir leads to overtures being made to William of Orange.

1688   William lands at Torbay. James flees to France.

1689   13 February: William and Mary proclaimed joint sovereigns of England. James lands in Ireland and begins campaign against Protestants.

The 1689 Rebellion

1689   April: William and Mary proclaimed joint sovereigns of Scotland by Scottish Convention. John Graham of Claverhouse, Viscount Dundee, rides north to raise Highlands for James II. 18 May: Western clans rally to Dundee at Dalcomera on River Lochy. Dundee requests Irish troops from James but only 300 sent under Colonel Cannon. June–July: Dundee, his force reduced by desertions to just over 2,000, advances from Lochaber to Blair Castle in Perthshire. From Edinburgh, General Mackay moves north with six Government regiments.

John Graham of Claverhouse, Viscount Dundee (1649–89), who led the 1689 rebellion and fell at Killiecrankie. (National Galleries of Scotland)

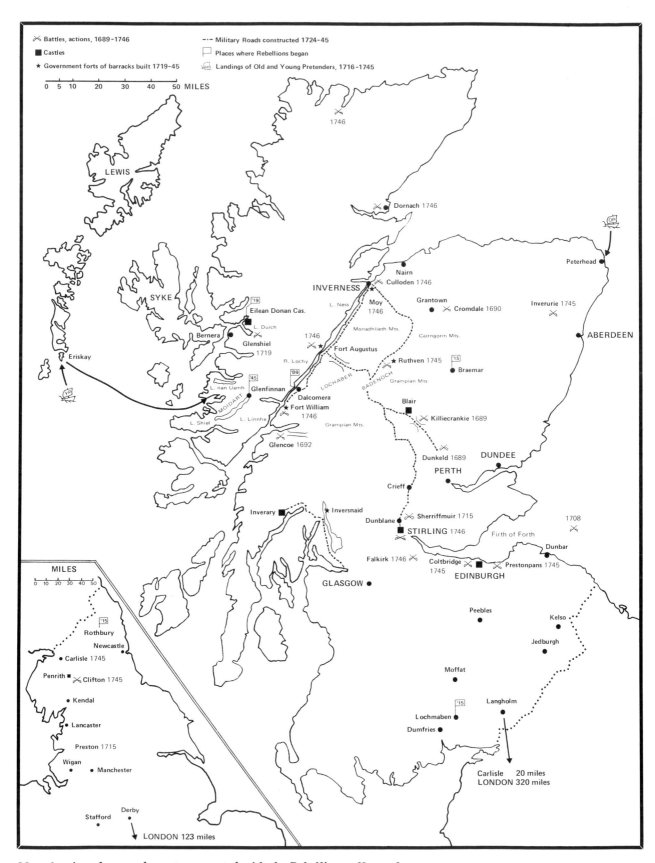

Key (top left):

⚔ Battles, actions, 1689-1746
■ Castles
★ Government forts of barracks built 1719-45
–·– Military Roads constructed 1724-45
☐ Places where Rebellions began
⛵ Landings of Old and Young Pretenders, 1716-1745

Scale: 0 5 10 20 30 40 50 MILES

Map labels:

LEWIS

SYKE

1746

Dornach 1746

Nairn
INVERNESS
Culloden 1746

Peterhead

[19] Eilean Donan Cas.
L. Duich
Bernera
Glenshiel
1719

L. Ness
Moy
1746
Grantown
Cromdale 1690
Inverurie 1745

ABERDEEN

1746
Fort Augustus
Monadhliath Mts.
Cairngorm Mts.

Eriskay
R. Lochy
[89]
LOCHABER
Ruthven 1745
[15]
Braemar

[45]
L. nan Uamh
Glenfinnan
Dalcomera
Fort William
1746
MOIDART
L. Shiel   L. Linnhe
Glencoe 1692

BADENOCH
Grampian Mts.

Blair
Killiecrankie 1689

Grampian Mts.
Dunkeld 1689
DUNDEE
PERTH

Crieff

Inverary
Inversnaid

Dunblane
Sherriffmuir 1715
STIRLING 1746

1708

Falkirk 1746
Coltbridge
1745
Dunbar
Prestonpans 1745
EDINBURGH
Firth of Forth

GLASGOW

Peebles
Kelso
Jedburgh
Moffat
Langholm
[15]
Lochmaben
Dumfries

Carlisle   20 miles
LONDON 320 miles

Inset (bottom left):

MILES
0 10 20 30 40 50

[15]
Rothbury
Newcastle
Carlisle 1745
Penrith   Clifton 1745
Kendal
Lancaster
Preston 1715
Wigan   Manchester

Stafford   Derby
LONDON 123 miles

Map showing places and events connected with the Rebellions, 1689-1746.

27 July: Battle of Killiecrankie. The armies meet just north of the Pass of Killiecrankie. Highland charge completely routs Mackay's regiments except for two, which retreat in good order to Stirling. Dundee killed and succeeded in command by Cannon. Highland army reinforced at Blair by fresh clans, but unity of purpose deteriorates under Cannon's poor leadership. Mackay regroups his forces.

18 August: Battle of Dunkeld. Jacobite army attacks Dunkeld held by Angus's Regiment (Cameronians). After four-hour struggle Highlanders routed and clans disperse. Chiefs sign a bond to support James II.

1690 William III begins major campaign against James in Ireland.

April: Cannon and Major-General Buchan from Ireland again summon clans but only 1,500 come out.

1 May: Mackay's dragoons rout Cannon and Buchan at Haughs of Cromdale, near Grantown-on-Spey.

June–July: Mackay marches 6,000 men through Highlands. Begins construction of Fort William at Inverlochy on Loch Linnhe to pacify region.

A late 17th-century army on the march in winter: a modern painting by C.C.P. Lawson. (National Army Museum)

1 July: In Ireland, William defeats James at Battle of the Boyne.

18 July: Mackay withdraws southwards, leaving garrison at Fort William under Colonel Hill.

1691 Hill maintains peace in Highlands.

17 August: William offers pardon to all chiefs who take oath of allegiance to him by 1 January. No chiefs begin to do so until December, when they receive James's permission.

December: Earl of Stair, Secretary of State for Scotland, plans to make an example of recalcitrant clans and moves more troops to Fort William.

30 December: MacIain, chief of Jacobite MacDonalds of Glencoe, arrives at Fort William to swear allegiance but told he can only do so at Inverary.

1692 6 January: MacIain takes the oath.

16 January: Stair orders destruction of MacDonalds of Glencoe.

1 February: Two companies of Argyll's Regiment under Captain Campbell of Glenlyon march from Fort William to Glencoe, where they are given shelter.

5

'The Highland Chieftain', a contemporary painting by Michael Wright, showing Highland dress *c.* 1660. The belted plaid is in several shades of red and brown with crimson and black stripes. The hose is black and red with gold garters. The slashed doublet is buff, richly embroidered in gold. Note the broadsword, dirk, pistol and gilt-studded bandolier with brass powder charges. The sword belt is buff, edged with gold lace. (National Galleries of Scotland)

13 February: The Massacre of Glencoe. Glenlyon's troops fall upon MacDonalds, but only succeed in killing a tenth of them, including MacIain.

Highlands now quiet. Rebellion in Ireland over. Jacobite hopes further dashed by destruction of French invasion fleet by Admiral Rooke in May off Cap de la Hague. Efforts now confined to assassination plots against William.

1693–97 William's war with France in the Low Countries ends with Peace of Ryswick.

1701 Death of James II. Louis XIV recognises his son, James Edward Stuart, as James III of England and VIII of Scotland (the Old Pretender). War of the Spanish Succession begins.

1702 William III dies and is succeeded by Queen Anne.

1707 Act of Union between Crowns of England and Scotland approved by both Parliaments.

The 1708 Rebellion

1708 February: French fleet and army of 6,000 assembled at Channel Ports for expedition to Scotland in support of Jacobites and to create diversion after Marlborough's successes in Low Countries.

March: Fleet sails with Pretender on board, but due to contrary winds and Royal Navy off the Firth of Forth, fails to land and returns to France.

1708–13 War of Spanish Succession continues and ends with Peace of Utrecht.

1714 Queen Anne dies without heirs, and is succeeded by Protestant Elector of Hanover, great-grandson of James I, as George I. Stuart claims to throne gain some support in England and much in Scotland, particularly in Highlands in opposition to Duke of Argyll's support for Hanoverian succession.

The 1715 Rebellion

1715 September–October: Pretender's standard raised at Braemar by Earl of Mar. Jacobites capture Inverness and Perth but fail to take Edinburgh Castle. By early October Mar's strength totals 1,000 horse and 5,000 foot, with 2,500 of western clans marching to join, plus 3,600 more expected from north. French landings, with Pretender, anticipated in Scotland and in Cornwall. Smaller Jacobite forces forming in northern England under Earl of Derwentwater and Thomas Forster and in Scottish borders under Lords Nithsdale, Kenmuir and Carnwath. Government forces in Scotland increased to five regiments of dragoons and five of foot, which concentrate at Stirling under Duke of Argyll.

9 October: Mar sends 2,000 men, mostly Highlanders, under Macintosh of Borlum to join English and Border Jacobites. Borlum crosses Firth of Forth to outflank Argyll at Stirling and threatens Edinburgh and Leith.

14 October: Argyll returns to Edinburgh with reinforcements.

16–18 October: Mar advances from Perth to Dunblane. Argyll returns to Stirling and Mar retreats to Perth to await reinforcements from north and west.

19–22 October: Borlum moves south and links up with English and Border Jacobites at Kelso. Southern Jacobite army now 600 horse and 1,400 foot.

27 October: Hearing that General Carpenter was advancing north from Newcastle with 1,000 troops, southern Jacobites march south-west towards Langholm.

30 October: Carpenter reaches Jedburgh. Jacobites decide to invade England in anticipation of support in Lancashire.

31 October–10 November: Advance continues through Kendal and Lancaster to Preston. Carpenter returns to Newcastle and moves south-west across Pennines on Preston.

4–5 November: Mar's army at Perth joined by 2,500 from western clans and 2,000 from north under Lord Seaforth.

10–12 November: General Wills in Cheshire with four regiments of dragoons and one of foot marches to Wigan, picking up another regiment of horse. Southern Jacobites at Preston learn of Wills's approach and decide to fight. Mar leaves Perth to advance across Forth, east of Stirling. Reaches Kinbuck, north of Dunblane, where Argyll arrives on 12th.

12 November: Battle of Preston. Wills, with 1,600 troops, attacks town from north-west and south-east. Jacobites hold out, but with Carpenter arriving on 13th, they surrender on 14th.

13 November: Battle of Sherriffmuir. Argyll, with five regiments of dragoons (900) and eight of foot (2,200), confronts Mar's 900 horse and 6,200 foot on Sherriffmuir, east of Dunblane. Mar's right wing attacks and routs Argyll's left, but his left wing is re-

Reconstruction of a Musketeer of the Earl of Angus's Regiment (26th Foot), which held Dunkeld in 1689. See also Plate B2. Statuette by C. Pilkington Jackson in the Scottish United Services Museum. (National Army Museum photo)

pulsed, counter-attacked successfully by Argyll's dragoons and beaten from the field. Mar's right (4,000) and Argyll's right (1,000) re-form and confront each other. Though Mar has advantage of ground and numbers, he fails to attack. Oncoming darkness ends battle. Though indecisive, Argyll has foiled Mar's attempt to move south. Argyll regroups at Dunblane. Mar, with many Highlanders desert-

ing, returns to Perth. On same day, Earl of Sutherland, with northern clans loyal to Government, recaptures Inverness from Jacobites.

Late November–early December: Mar's strength falls from desertion to about 4,000. Argyll's increases.

22 December: Pretender lands in Scotland near Aberdeen, falls ill and does not reach Perth until 9 January. Argyll at Stirling reinforced to seven regiments of cavalry and 12 of foot. Prepares advance to Perth.

1716 Late January: Jacobites burn Perthshire villages to impede Argyll's advance.

William III's infantry and artillery in action at the Battle of the Boyne, 1690. The regiment advancing from the left is headed by its grenadiers, led by an officer carrying a fusil. Detail of a contemporary painting by Jan Wyck. (National Army Museum)

30 January–2 February: Jacobites retreat from Perth towards Dundee, pursued by Argyll.

4 February: Pretender embarks for France.

5–12 February: Jacobites continue retreat to Aberdeen, then move west to Ruthven in Badenoch, where clans disperse home in mid-February. Argyll halts at Aberdeen.

March–April: Government troops police Badenoch and Lochaber. Garrison of seven regiments of dragoons and 21 of foot left in Scotland north of line Edinburgh-Glasgow. Steps taken to disarm and pacify clans but hampered by inaccessibility of Highlands. Estates of prominent Jacobites forfeited. Government reprisals relatively light in Scotland but severe on English Jacobites.

1717 Duke of Orleans, Regent of France for infant Louis XV, seeks better relations with Britain and requires Old Pretender to leave France for Italy. Charles XII of Sweden, eager for revenge on George I for loss of territory to Hanover, offers military aid to restore Stuarts, but plot discovered.

1718 British naval operations to halt Spanish aggression in Mediterranean lead to Spain becoming chief hope of Jacobites. Philip V's chief minister, Cardinal Alberoni, plots with Jacobite Duke of Ormonde to land 5,000 men in England while diversion made in Scotland under George Keith, Earl Marischal. Plans leaked to Britain by France and counter-preparations made.

The 1719 Rebellion

1719 7 March: Main Spanish expedition sails from Cadiz.

8 March: Old Pretender arrives in Spain. Marischal sails for Scotland from St Sebastian with arms, ammunition, money and 300 Spanish troops.

19 March: Leading Jacobites in

General Hugh Mackay of Scourie (1640–92), commander of the Government troops in the 1689 Rebellion. After Sir Godfrey Kneller. (National Army Museum)

France, though disunited over choice of leadership between Marischal and Marquis of Tullibardine, sail for Scotland to rendezvous with Marischal on Isle of Lewis.

29 March: Main Spanish expedition scattered by storms and returns to Spain.

4 April: Jacobites link up on Lewis. Marischal resigns command to Tullibardine but retains control of ships. All sail for west coast.

13 April: Expedition establishes headquarters at Eilean Donan Castle on Loch Duich in Kintail. Plans to attack Inverness discussed but discarded. News of failure of Spanish fleet received.

Late April: Government reinforces Inverness garrison. Five Royal Naval ships block Jacobite escape route by sea.

10 May: Warships blow up Eilean

Donan. Tullibardine tries to raise clans but only 1,500 come out.

5 June: General Wightman marches from Inverness for Kintail with 1,100 troops: four regiments of foot, one squadron of dragoons and some Government Highlanders.

10 June: Battle of Glenshiel. Wightman attacks Jacobites and Spaniards holding pass leading to Kintail. Troops rout Highlanders on left and attack Spaniards in centre, who retreat to another position. Left without support, they surrender the next day. Highlanders disperse, Marischal and Tullibardine escape and eventually reach Continent.

1720   Heir, Charles Edward, born to Old Pretender in Italy (the Young Pretender).

1720–40   House of Hanover, with George II succeeding in 1727, now accepted in England and much of Scotland. Stuart hopes diminish. In Scotland, General Wade pacifies Highlands by raising independent companies of Government Highlanders, confiscating arms and opening up inaccessible regions with roads. Fort William strengthened and further forts built at Inverness, Killiechuimen (later Fort Augustus), Bernera, opposite Skye in Kintail, Ruthven and Inversnaid in Argyllshire. In 1739 the Highland Regiment

Infantry of William III's army in action led by grenadiers; compare their caps with those of the 18th century. A modern painting by C.C.P. Lawson. (National Army Museum)

(Black Watch) is formed. With many Jacobite leaders abroad and those in Scotland fearful of another failure, Highlands remain quiet.

1741 War of the Austrian Succession begins over Prussia's attack on Austria. Britain sides with Austria, France with Prussia.

1743 Battle of Dettingen. British army under George II defeats French in Germany. France sees Jacobites as means of weakening Britain. Old Pretender, now 60, disinclined for further adventure but Prince Charles Edward, now 24, eager for action.

1744 Prince travels secretly to join French fleet and army assembling at Dunkirk for invasion of England. Storm ruins fleet before it can sail. Project abandoned and troops transferred to Flanders. Prince remains in France, but no French help now forthcoming. Jacobite agents sound out chances of rising in Scotland.

1745 11 May: Battle of Fontenoy. French defeat Duke of Cumberland's Allied army. Jacobite hopes rise.

5 July: Prince sails from France for Scotland with seven followers, arms and ammunition and two ships. One ship and most of arms lost when attacked by HMS *Lion* off Cornwall, but Prince sails on.

23 July: Prince lands on Isle of Eriskay in Outer Hebrides.

The 1745 Rebellion

1745 25 July: Prince lands on west coast at Loch nan Uamh near Moidart. Arrival announced to traditionally Jacobite western clans, but most are reluctant to come out without French support. Cameron of Locheil and Macdonald of Keppoch promise aid.

6 August: Prince writes to Louis XV for help.

19 August: Prince's standard raised at Glenfinnan on Loch Shiel. Joined by some 1,000 clansmen of Locheil's and

A portrait by Richard Waitt of Kenneth, 3rd Lord Duffus, who was an active Jacobite in the '15. The slashed doublet is red with gold buttons. The belted plaid and hose are black, red, yellow and white. Pistol, dirk and sporran all hang from the waist belt supporting the plaid. From the strap over the left shoulder hang a powder charge, priming flask and pickers. A blue bonnet with white feather is in the left hand. (National Galleries of Scotland)

Keppoch's. Other Macdonalds and Appin Stewarts join later.

21–29 August: Prince marches east, passing between Forts William and Augustus, towards Corrieyairack Pass. General Cope, commanding in Scotland, marching north from Stirling with 2,000 men for Fort Augustus via Corrieyairack, reaches Crieff; continues march and learns that Jacobites hold Corrieyairack. Changes plan and makes forced march to Inverness. Prince crosses pass to attack Cope but, finding him gone, turns south. Camerons attack Ruthven Barracks but repulsed by small detachment of Guise's Regiment (6th Foot).

William Cumming, piper to the Laird of Grant, 1714, by Richard Waitt. *Bonnet:* dark brown, scarlet cockade and brow band. *Jacket:* scarlet, silver and pale green embroidery. *Plaid:* red and grey stripes, yellow lines edged black. *Hose:* red and grey on golden yellow ground. *Baldrick:* brown cloth, green fringe. *Pipes:* silver mounted, buff bag, crimson cords, white banner fringed red and white, Grant arms in red. Note the targe slung over the left shoulder. Although Clan Grant favoured the Government, the dress is typical for the period. **(National Galleries of Scotland)**

30 August–4 September: Prince marches to Blair Castle and Perth. Receives reinforcements and appoints Duke of Perth and Lord George Murray joint lieutenant-generals of his army. Cope at Inverness learns of Prince's moves. Marches to Aberdeen to await ships to move troops to Edinburgh.

11–16 September: Prince, now 2,400 strong, marches from Perth to outskirts of Edinburgh, bypassing Stirling held by Government garrison and routing two regiments of dragoons at Coltbridge.

17 September: Prince takes Edinburgh, but Castle remains in Government hands. Proclaims James III king with himself as Regent. Cope disembarks troops at Dunbar, east of city.

19 September: Cope moves west to Haddington. Prince moves east to Duddington.

20 September: Cope, with four regiments of foot and two of dragoons (2,100 men), takes up position on coast near Prestonpans facing south, his front protected by a morass. Jacobites, 2,300 strong, form on high ground to south.

21 September: Battle of Prestonpans. During darkness Jacobite army guided across morass to a position opposite Cope's left flank. At daybreak Lord George Murray attacks from east. Cope changes front, but his inexperienced troops are routed within ten minutes. Cope flees to Berwick. Prince returns to Edinburgh.

October: Prince's army recruited to 5,000 foot and 500 horse, organized and trained by Lord George Murray. Future plans discussed. In England troops assemble at Newcastle under Wade. Cumberland and regiments from Flanders recalled to concentrate in Midlands. Militia called out and new regiments raised. In Highlands loyal clans form new regiments: Loudon's, Argyll Militia and 18 new independent companies.

1–17 November: Jacobite army leaves Edinburgh for Carlisle in two columns: one under Perth and Tullibardine marching to Moffat and Peebles; second under Prince and Murray to Kelso and Jedburgh. Carlisle is besieged and capitulates. Wade sends two regiments of foot and two of dragoons north to re-occupy Edinburgh, then marches west from Newcastle on 16th. Finds roads impassable and returns.

20–29 November: Jacobites continue

to Manchester via Preston in hope of finding support in Lancashire. None forthcoming except for 200 recruits in Manchester.

1–4 December: Main army marches to Derby while Murray feints west to draw off Cumberland, then in Staffordshire with 2,000 horse and 8,000 foot. Murray succeeds in inducing Cumberland to move north to Stafford and rejoins Prince in Derby.

5–6 December: At Derby. Prince keen to press on to London, then strengthening its defences, but with Wade advancing again from Newcastle and Cumberland to west, other leaders counsel retreat to Scotland, where some French troops had been landed and fresh recruits raised. In northern Scotland Lord Loudon begins operations against Jacobite clans.

7 December: Retreat from Derby begins. Prince in low spirits; discipline and morale deteriorate.

8–16 December: Retreat continues to Penrith via Wigan and Kendal. Cumberland marches to overtake and Wade tries to intercept, but misses Jacobites at Wigan. In the north, Loudon occupies Inverness and imprisons Lord Lovat.

17 December: Action at Clifton. Murray with Highland rearguard successfully fights off Cumberland's advance guard.

20 December: Jacobites march from Carlisle into Scotland, leaving the Manchester regiment and some non-clan troops (400) to hold the castle.

21–30 December: Jacobites reach Glasgow on Christmas Day. Cumberland besieges Carlisle, which surrenders on 30th, and returns to London, leaving General Hawley to pursue the Jacobites. French invasion scare in south-east England.

1746 1–16 January: Jacobites, reinforced to 9,000 strong, besiege Stirling Castle. Hawley concentrates his force at Edin-

The Laird of Grant's Champion, Alastair Grant Mor, 1714, by Richard Waitt. His bonnet and plaid, which match the hose, are similar to the piper's. The jacket is blue but may once have been green, the waistcoat red. Sporran and targe are pale brown leather, latter with brass studs. The curved sword is most unusual. (The Earl of Seafield)

burgh with troops already there plus Wade's from Newcastle, making three regiments of dragoons and 14 of foot. On 14th marches with 7,000 to relieve Stirling via Linlithgow and Falkirk. Murray advances to oppose Hawley, leaving 1,000 before Stirling.

17 January: Battle of Falkirk. Murray takes up position on high ground. Hawley has to advance uphill into wind and rain. His dragoons charge but are repulsed. Clan regiments in Murray's front line charge Hawley's infantry. Latter break except for two regiments on right wing which open fire on Jacobite left before retiring in good order. Indiscipline of Highlanders prevents Murray from exploiting

13

Landing of James Edward Stuart, the Old Pretender, in Scotland, 1716. Contemporary engraving by Schenk. (National Galleries of Scotland)

victory. Hawley regroups and retreats to Edinburgh. Jacobites return to besiege Stirling.

18–28 January: Siege makes no progress. Many Highlanders desert. Cumberland posts north to take command in Scotland and reaches Edinburgh on 30th.

29 January: Murray and clan chiefs inform Prince of desertions, futility of continuing siege and danger of remaining at Stirling. Recommend retreat into Highlands for winter and capture of Highland forts. Prince reluctantly agrees. His relations with Murray, never good, deteriorate further.

1 February: Jacobites march north for Inverness in two columns.

4 February: Cumberland begins pursuit north. Loudon fortifies Inverness against Jacobite advance.

6 February: Cumberland reaches Perth but halted by bad weather. 5,000 Hessian troops reach Edinburgh.

16 February: Loudon's attempt to seize Prince at Moy Castle, seven miles south of Inverness, fails.

18 February: Loudon, outnumbered by advancing Jacobites, abandons Inverness and retreats north to Dornoch in Sutherland.

19–20 February: Jacobite army concentrates at Inverness.

25 February: Cumberland reaches Aberdeen and decides to wait for better weather and retrain his troops. Hessians left to garrison Perth area.

March: Two clan regiments with French troops capture Fort Augustus but fail to take Fort William. Earl of Cromarty, later joined by Murray and Perth, moves against Loudon in Sutherland, taking Dornoch and 300 prisoners. Loudon escapes west with some independent companies to Skye. Murray returns and raids Blair Castle.

Mackay's Independent Company surprise French detachment landing arms and treasure on north-west coast.

8 April: Cumberland marches from Aberdeen. Outlying detachments of Jacobites recalled to Inverness. Force at Fort William abandon siege and rejoin, but Cromarty's men routed by independent companies in Sutherland.

14 April: Cumberland reaches Nairn. Jacobites advance to Culloden and take position on Drummossie Moor. Many men desert to find food.

15 April: Jacobites march by night to surprise Cumberland. More desert; march discipline is poor, and dawn appears before Nairn can be reached. Murray overrules Prince and orders retreat. Men exhausted and near-starving on return to Culloden.

16 April: Battle of Culloden. Disregarding Murray's advice, Prince adopts position on open ground on Drummossie Moor. Army just under 5,000 strong. Cumberland's army,

The Battle of Glenshiel, 1719. Note the 2nd Dragoons (Scots Greys) with Spanish prisoners in the foreground. A modern reconstruction by Lionel Edwards which gives an accurate representation of the terrain at the site of the battle. (National Army Museum)

three regiments of dragoons, 15 of foot, Argyll Militia and 10 guns, nearly 9,000 strong, march from Nairn and confront Jacobites. Cumberland's guns open fire. Clans in right centre charge, followed by right wing. Attack held by Cumberland's infantry on left and attacked in flank by dragoons and Argyll Militia. Front line clan regiments give way and retreat, covered by second line. Prince flees and army dissolves, rigorously pursued by dragoons. Cumberland enters Inverness. Some clansmen rally with Perth and Murray at Ruthven to await Prince. Latter never comes and clans disperse.

Aftermath

April September: Cumberland stamps out all vestiges of rebellion in

Highlands with great severity. Many prisoners executed, others transported to colonies. In July Cumberland returns to Flanders campaign with part of his army. Prince hunted unsuccessfully all over Western Highlands and Islands with price of £30,000 on his head.

19 September: Prince sails from Loch nan Uamh for France.

1746–48 Parliament passes laws to break down clan system, destroy feudal power of chiefs, forbid possession of arms and wearing of Highland dress.

1748 War of Austrian Succession ends.

1752 Discovery of Jacobite plot to assassinate Royal Family and seize power in London, followed by landing of Swedish force in Scotland.

1760 Accession of George III.

1766 Old Pretender dies.

1788 Young Pretender dies. His brother, Henry, Cardinal of York, now surviving Stuart claimant; dies 1807.

The Jacobite Forces

Between the first Jacobite rising in 1689 and the final collapse of the cause in 1746, the hopes of the House of Stuart were centred chiefly on Scotland, the country from which it had sprung. Though there were many influential people in England with Jacobite sympathies, few were prepared to hazard their positions; only in the '15 did English Jacobites take the field to any significant extent, and even then their support proved far less than anticipated. Although the first two Georges were never popular in England, fears of a Roman Catholic monarchy, the threat of civil war, the repugnance of English people at the thought of foreign troops on British soil, the sight of the two Pretenders' Highland troops, regarded by most English as little more than alien savages, plus the increasing prosperity and stability of the early 18th century, all combined to convince the population that their German monarchs were preferable to anything the Stuarts could offer.

Furthermore it would be quite wrong to regard the Jacobite rebellions as a contest between England and Scotland. In the 17th and 18th centuries the Lowland Scots shared many of the feelings of the English, and had cause to hate and fear their fellow countrymen in the Highlands. Indeed some of the most brutal treatment inflicted on rebellious Highlanders after the '45 was the work of Lowland Scots. Although there were noblemen in the Scottish borders and southwest, as well as the lowlands of the north and north-east, who came out in the '15 and the '45, they were the exceptions rather than the rule. Thus it was upon the Highland clans that the Jacobites relied for their most reliable manpower; but even these were by no means unanimous in their support for the Stuart cause.

Major James Fraser of Castle Leather, wearing tartan jacket and trews in red and green with thin black lines. The plaid is predominantly red with green stripes and white lines. The garters are red. Sword belt, black leather. Fraser was a Government supporter, but the dress is typical of the first two decades of the 18th century. (Miss Fiona Fraser)

A German engraving showing how the belted plaid was worn. The figures are Government Highlanders but the arrangement of the plaid would be the same for Jacobites. (National Army Museum)

Clan Campbell, the most powerful in the Highlands and determined to retain its power, traditionally sided with the ruling monarch, be he Dutch William or Hanoverian George; only once did a Campbell chief lose his head for opposition to his king, and that was against the Stuart, James II. Clan Campbell's loyalty was rewarded by the successive elevation of their chiefs from the rank of earl to duke. Their example was followed by smaller clans of the northern and central Highlands, e.g. the Grants, Munros, Rosses, Mackays and Sutherlands. The Macleods and Mackenzies in the west, though Jacobite in the '15 and '19, gave their loyalty to the Crown in the '45, as did the Sleat branch of the traditionally Jacobite Macdonalds.

Religion too played its part, those clans which were Presbyterian inclining to the House of Hanover, and those which were Catholic or Episcopalian to the Stuarts. The latter came predominantly from the West Highlands: the various Macdonalds, once the most numerous and powerful before the Campbells began their ascendancy, and the Camerons, Macleans and Stewarts of Appin. Even among these allegiance was determined more by hatred of Clan Campbell than by the desire to see a Stuart king in distant Whitehall.

As for the ordinary clansman, his personal inclinations to Hanover or Stuart, if he had any, counted for little. He obeyed his feudal chief, either out of personal devotion to him, or because he feared the consequences to his home and family if he did not. The ranks of Highland armies were filled by fear of burning crofts. Nevertheless, once in the field, many clansmen fought with devotion and loyalty, particularly when they had sight of or contact with the man for whom they were fighting, as was seen in the '45 and its aftermath. On the other hand, they could not always be relied upon when things went ill, and desertion was one of the biggest handicaps suffered by a Highland army.

The feudal nature and rigid structure of the Highland clan, under a chief with absolute power over life and death, allied to the warlike nature, skill-at-arms and fierce pride of every member from the highest to the lowest, made it an organisation rapidly adaptable to war. When the call to arms came, the clan turned itself into a regiment: the chief became its colonel, his sons and kinsmen, who were his tenants or tacksmen, its officers, their tenants its NCOs, and their sub-tenants the rank and file. When the clan formed for battle it faced the enemy according to the social standing of its members, with the officers leading, the superior men in the front ranks, grading back to the impoverished and landless— the common 'humblies'—in the rear. This ranking by comparative wealth and status ensured that the better-armed and those most likely to possess powers of leadership would always be in front.

The chief and his tacksmen would probably have the full complement of Highland weapons: the broadsword, the 18-inch dirk, a brace of pistols, a long firearm, and the leather-covered, circular wooden shield known as a targe. The front-rank men would probably have some, if not all of these, while the humblies in the rear might have only a dirk, a club, a hay fork, or perhaps the cutting blade mounted on a long pole, which was known as a Lochaber axe. Some

Highland weapons of the 18th century: two broadswords, dirks, pistols, targe and powder flask. (National Museum of Antiquities of Scotland)

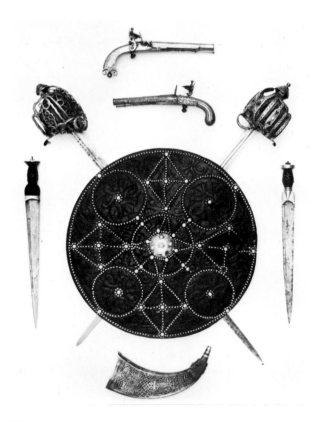

regiments were so poorly armed that the rearmost ranks had only sticks, while before Prestonpans some of the Duke of Perth's non-clan regiment had to be equipped with scythe blades attached to poles—which in fact inflicted fearful execution. However, from Killiecrankie to Culloden, the strength of the Jacobite infantry lay predominantly in its swordsmen.

In the early 17th century and before, the favoured weapon had been the great, two-handed sword, the 'claidheamh mor' or claymore, which had a hilt some 15 inches long, a drooping cross-guard and a straight blade some 3ft. 7ins. in length. Some of these may have been used at Killiecrankie, but during the 17th century they were generally superseded by the basket-hilted broadsword, the blades of many being cut down from old claymores. The basket hilt originated on the Continent, whence it was adopted in England during the Civil War for use by cavalry, and indeed continued as the cavalryman's sword until well into the 18th century. Whether the Scots took it up through contact with Cromwellian horse, or acquired it straight from the Continent, seems uncertain. In any event, it had become the Highlander's prime weapon by the late 17th century. He confronted his foe with broadsword in right hand, dirk in his left, and targe on his left forearm. In the '45 a much greater proportion of clansmen than before had muskets, the best of which were of French or Spanish manufacture, the native variety often being old and unserviceable. Even so, due to the overall shortage of ammunition, each man on average having only 12 rounds, the clansman still relied on the sword, rather than musketry, to overcome his enemies.

A common fallacy about the Highlanders who filled the ranks of Jacobite armies suggests they were all strong, tall men in the prime of life. In fact statistics of physical details of Jacobite prisoners taken in the '45 show that the average height was only 5ft. 4ins. As for age and physique, it must be remembered that the clan system required all men to follow their chief; the age scale ran from lads of 15 or 16 to men in their sixties, or even seventies, and the lists of prisoners include madmen, the deaf, dumb and blind, the club-footed, and sundry other defectives. On the other hand, the rigours of their normal existence and climate bred a race that had to be tough and hardy to survive.

In Dundee's rebellion and the '15 the men of one clan would normally fight together as a body, regardless of their numbers, so that the individual components of a Jacobite army in those rebellions might vary considerably in strength. Such armies were really no more than a tribal horde, though perhaps more so in 1689 than 1715. In the '45, when Lord George Murray endeavoured to impose a more regular organisation upon the Prince's army, with proper rank designations and even pay for the men, those clans which were weak in numbers, either through lack of manpower, desertion from the ranks or divided loyalties, were regimented with others to form a more viable unit. Thus the only regiment raised by a woman, Lady Mackintosh's, included her own people, M'Gillivrays, Farquharsons and M'Beans; the Macdonalds of Glencoe, only 120 strong, were merged with Macdonald of Keppoch's; and the MacLeans and MacLachlans, though originally forming two regiments, were combined into one at Culloden.

Dundee's army, apart from a small group of horse, of which more later, and some of James II's Irish troops, was entirely formed of Highlanders. In the '15 and the '45, though the chief strength and the first line of the armies were composed of clan regiments, there were also other, non-clan units. These were recruited either from Highland or near-Highland areas, or from Highlanders owing no particular allegiance to any chief, such as the Atholl Brigade and Gordon of Glenbucket's, or from low-country districts north of Edinburgh like Aberdeenshire and Angus, which provided regiments like Lord Ogilvy's, Lord Lewis Gordon's and the Duke of Perth's. The latter was also partly recruited in Edinburgh, as was Roy Stuart's. The true Lowlands of Scotland, the Border country south of Edinburgh and the south-west, contributed some horse in the '15 but little or nothing in the '45. English participation was confined, in the '15, to some horse and a few 'Lancashire rustics, an uncouth and unsoldierlike body ... some with rusty swords, others with muskets, some with fowling pieces, others with pitchforks'. The '45

A romanticised version of Prince Charles Edward Stuart, the Young Pretender, taking leave of Antoine Walsh, captain of the 'Doutelle' which brought him to Scotland from France. Although the Prince is shown in Highland dress with belted plaid, he in fact landed dressed in black. He wore tartan clothing during the Rebellion but did not adopt the kilt until he was a fugitive. (National Galleries of Scotland)

saw the inclusion in the Duke of Perth's and Roy Stuart's of some English deserters and prisoners taken at Prestonpans, and the raising for the Prince of the pathetic Manchester Regiment, never more than 300 strong, which was abandoned to its grim fate in Carlisle after the retreat from Derby.

The third and smallest element of the Jacobite infantry were the contingents of foreign regular soldiers: in the '19 from Spain and in 1746 from the Scots and Irish regiments in the French service, plus some individual officers and a few gunners. In both rebellions the numbers that actually arrived in Scotland were less than those despatched. Only 300 Spanish infantry took part in the '19, and in 1746 about 300 of the 'Royal-Écossais' and rather less of three Irish regiments (Dillon's, Ruth's and Lally's) fought in Scotland.

Cavalry was by far the weakest arm of Jacobite forces, only surpassed in feebleness—almost non-existence—by their artillery. In 1689 Dundee could only muster some 40 horsemen, who nevertheless were effective against Mackay's two troops

The Battle of Prestonpans, 1745; a print from a 19th-century painting by Sir William Allen. The Highlanders are more of the artist's period than the '45. (National Army Museum)

and in the pursuit after Killiecrankie. The two Jacobite armies of the '15 mustered between them three main types. With Mar in the north there was a small body of Highlanders mounted on rough ponies with slung muskets. With Derwentwater and Forster there were numerous English gentlemen with their tenants and servants—'fox-hunters armed with light dress swords'. The largest element and probably the best were the troops of Lowland horse raised by noblemen in Aberdeenshire, Stirlingshire, Fife and Angus with Mar's army, and those from the south-west with Forster. However, even these troopers had little effect on the outcome of the campaign; at Sherriffmuir the performance of the Jacobite horse was distinguished first by getting itself into the wrong position, and second by its inactivity at two crucial stages of the battle. The cavalry of the '45 consisted, at its greatest strength, of two troops of Life Guards and three other troops, each averaging about 90 men. The Life Guards and Kilmarnock's troop were largely made up of gentlemen and their servants. The most effective at patrolling and outpost duties was the troop of hussars led by John Baggot, an Irish officer in the French service. Great difficulty was encountered in finding sufficient horses to keep all these troops mounted, particularly after the retreat back to Scotland, and before Culloden many of the surviving horses were handed over to the Franco-Scots squadron of Fitzjames' Horse, which had arrived from France dismounted.

The inability of the Jacobite horse, through lack of numbers, training and suitable horses, to influence decisively the outcome of a set-piece battle, as would regular cavalry, was to some extent immaterial since the tactics of its foot were akin to a cavalry charge. When about to give battle a Jacobite force would endeavour to deploy on high ground of its own choosing, as was done successfully at Killiecrankie, Sherriffmuir, Prestonpans and Falkirk. There the army would be formed for battle, usually in two lines with any cavalry on either flank. The clan regiments were almost invariably all in the first line; their relative positions in the line often being the occasion of much squabbling over ancient privileges. At Culloden, for instance, the Macdonalds, piqued at being deprived of what they regarded as their prerogative of the post of honour on the right flank, sulked on the left wing and refused to support the advance of the clans in the centre and right. The foreign troops were only trained according to the normal conventions of European warfare so that, in the only fighting when they were present, at Glenshiel in 1719 and in 1746, they were employed at the former to hold some entrenchments and in the latter as a reserve.

When all was ready—and sometimes before—the only tactic known to Jacobite forces would be

20

launched: the Highland charge. This was the same at Killiecrankie, though with fewer firearms available, as nearly 60 years later. After pulling their bonnets firmly down on their heads with 'an emphatic scrug' and, in the earlier days at least, discarding their plaids, the clans would surge forward 'like a living flood'. Each man would 'incline his body horizontally forward, cover it with his targe, rush to within fifty paces of the enemy's line, discharge and drop his musket; dart within twelve paces, discharge and fling his iron-stocked pistol at the foeman's head; draw broadsword and at him'. By the time they reached the enemy line they were in blocks or wedges, 12 or 14 deep. 'Stooping below the charged bayonets, they tossed them upwards by the targe, dirking the front rank man with the left hand, while stabbing or hewing down the rear rank man with the right.' Such an onset, delivered with great speed and courage, proved almost entirely successful at Killiecrankie, only two of Mackay's regiments holding their ground; partially so at Sherriffmuir; wholly so at Prestonpans and Falkirk, though at the latter two regiments stood firm; but failed at Culloden, where it was confronted by troops specially trained to meet it. It was, however, the clans' only tactic, and once it failed the battle was lost, owing to the Highlanders' inability to re-form and try again. This stemmed from their lack of discipline, which even in a victory like Falkirk made it impossible for a commander to regroup and pursue the defeated foe. The Highlander was keen to reap what loot he could from his successful charge and then make off home with it. Nor was their wild onslaught of any value to them when fighting in built-up areas. At Dunkeld in 1689 the clans were routed by a single, newly-raised regiment of foot, and at Preston in 1715 they were defeated by some dismounted dragoons and one regiment of foot, oddly enough the same that had prevailed at Dunkeld—a Lowland Scots corps, the Cameronians, 26th Foot.

Any attempt to alter their method of fighting and instil the rudiments of normal military organisation and discipline was fruitless, as Dundee discovered. Lord George Murray toiled endlessly to impose method, obedience to commands, and strict performance of duties, as the entries

Lord George Murray, lieutenant-general of the Prince's army, in Highland dress. The jacket is of a red, green, blue and black sett, the hose and waistcoat are of red and green stripes with thin black and blue lines. The belted plaid is green, blue and red. One of the figures in the background is dressed similarly to Murray, the other wears trews and a plaid. (The Duke of Atholl)

in the surviving order books show; but his days as the most able of the Jacobite generals were plagued by the Highlanders' inability to subdue their fierce pride to discipline, and by their propensity to desert in large numbers. It must be admitted, however, that this was due more to the urge to carry home booty or search for badly needed food than a lack of fighting spirit.

There is not space here to list in detail the component units of the various Jacobite armies from 1689 onwards, but there follows the composition of one of the best organised at the summit of its success— that of the Young Pretender as it left Edinburgh for the invasion of England on 1 November 1745. Some remarks about constitution of regiments, participation in earlier rebellions where known, and actions in the '45 are included.

Abbreviations: (c) = Clan regiment. Tp = Troop. Sqn = Squadron. Bn = Battalion. incl = Including, '89, '15, '19 = Out in 1689, 1715 and

1719 Rebellions. P = Prestonpans. F = Falkirk. N = Northern campaign against Loudon. C = Culloden.

Unit	Strength	Remarks
Troops of Horse		
1st Tp, Life Guards, Lord Elcho's	125	F, C.
2nd Tp, Life Guards, Lord Balmerino's	40	F, C.
Lord Kilmarnock's Horse Guards	100	Incl Strathallan's sqn. P, F, C.
Lord Pitsligo's Horse	120	F, C.
Baggot's Hussars	70	F, C.
Regiments of Foot		
Cameron of Locheil's (c)	740	'89, '15, '19. P, F, C.
Stewart of Appin's (c)	360	'15. P, F, C.
Atholl Brigade: Lord Geo. Murray's. 3 Bns: Lord Nairne's Mercer of Aldie's Menzies of Shian's	1,000	Incl Athollmen, Menzies & Robertsons. '15. P, F, C.
Macdonald of Clanranald's (c)	300	Incl Macdonalds of Kinlochmoidart & Morar. '89, '15. P, F, C.
Macdonald of Keppoch's (c)	400	Incl Macdonalds of Glencoe ('89, '15) & MacKinnons ('19). '15. P, F, C.
Macdonell of Glengarry's (c)	400?	'15, '19. P, F, C.
Gordon of Glenbucket's	427	'15. C.
Lord Ogilvy's or Angus	500	Later 2 bns. F, C.
Duke of Perth's	750	Incl some Macgregors ('15), Robertsons & Drummonds ('15). P, C.
MacLachlan of Castle Lachlan's(c)	260	P, C.
Macgregor of Glencarnock's (c)	300	'15, '19. P, F, N.
Roy Stuart's or Edinburgh	450	C.

Artillery

6 Swedish guns, 2 to 4 pdrs., French gunners.

6 1½-pdrs., taken at Prestonpans.

1 iron gun.

Total ration strength: 7,587 (including headquarters, miscellaneous small units and possibly followers).

Other regiments/clans active in Jacobite cause in the '45:

Chisholm of Strathglass's(c). C.

Earl of Cromarty's (Mackenzies)(c). '15, '19. F, N.

Lord Lewis Gordon's. F, C.

Farquharson of Monaltrie's. F. Merged with Ld Lewis Gordon's. C.

Grants of Glenmoriston and Glenurquhart. With Glengarry's. P, C. (Note: Most Grants were pro-Government.)

Lord Lovat's (Frasers)(c). '15 but deserted. F, N, C.

Macdonell of Barisdale's(c). P. Merged with Glengarry's.

Lady Mackintosh's. Incl M'Gillivrays, Farquharsons, M'Beans. F, N, C.

Maclarens(c). With Appin Stewarts. C.

Macpherson of Cluny's(c). F.

Macleods of Raasay(c). With Glengarry's. F.

MacLeans(c). '89, '15. Merged with MacLachlan's. C.

The Government Forces

Up to the Act of Union in 1707 the Crown maintained quite separate military establishments in England, Scotland and Ireland. Ever since the Restoration, Parliament had tried to reduce the King's permanent troops, but the threat posed by Monmouth's rebellion in 1685 had enabled James II to increase and strengthen his forces so that by 1688 the combined strength of the three armies was 34,000 men. James's talent as a military administrator had, up to a point, greatly improved the forces he had inherited from his brother, Charles II; but his motives in having a strong army—to consolidate his position as an absolute and Catholic monarch—entirely alienated a predominantly Protestant England, while his attempts to Catholicize the English Army by infiltrating Irish officers and men into its ranks lost him the loyalty of the force on which he depended to sustain his position. Thus, when the Protestant William of Orange was invited over from Holland in 1688 to assume the throne, James found himself abandoned by the English and Scots armies and fled the country.

William had seen the standing forces in Britain as a useful reinforcement for his struggle with Louis XIV, but he found them demoralised and of doubtful discipline following the uncertainties of the 'Glorious Revolution'. Furthermore, the all-pervading corruption of the times spilled over into the army, where commissions were bought and sold and regiments were virtually their colonels' private property, providing a valuable source of profit for the unscrupulous and opportunities for extortion by civilian officials of the Paymaster-General's department. The morale

and efficiency of honest officers and good soldiers became undermined, and the reputation of the army, never popular in England since Cromwell's rule, sank even lower in the eyes of the country, making the manning of its ranks, theoretically dependent on voluntary enlistment, increasingly difficult. The better type of man was loath to enlist, so that recourse had to be made to the poorest and often criminal classes of society.

Nevertheless William had to forge this dubious instrument into a formidable fighting force, for he had to contend not only with his Continental campaign against Louis XIV, but with the risings in Scotland and Ireland on behalf of James II. He had brought over from Holland some of his seasoned Dutch troops (which included a Scots Brigade that fought without distinction at Killiecrankie), and experienced Dutch generals. Gradually, after a shaky start, his English, Scots and Protestant Irish troops improved in quality through experience on the battlefield and the efforts of men like John Churchill, then Earl of Marlborough. By the close of William's Low Countries campaign in 1697 the British soldier had regained much of the high reputation enjoyed by his Cromwellian forebears.

Once peace was signed Parliament wasted no time in disbanding as much of William's army as it could get away with, so that, when the War of the Spanish Succession broke out in 1702, the

The grenadiers of Barrell's Regiment, 4th King's Own, meeting the onset of the Highlanders at Culloden. From the painting 'An Incident in the Rebellion of 1745' by David Morier. Although the sergeant (with waist sash and halbert) and the grenadiers wear caps, the two officers, one with a fusil, the other with a spontoon, are in hats. The sergeant has plain silver lace. The Jacobite figures were based on prisoners taken during the Rebellion. (Reproduced by gracious permission of H.M. The Queen)

William Augustus, Duke of Cumberland, commander of the King's forces in Scotland. Painting by John Wootton and Thomas Hudson. The Duke is portrayed at the Battle of Dettingen, 1743; he wears a scarlet coat faced blue, and scarlet waistcoat and breeches; all lace is gold. The horse furniture is blue and gold. (Reproduced by gracious permission of H.M. The Queen)

work of building up an army fit for war had to be done all over again. The same occurred after the Peace of Utrecht in 1713, leaving the magnificent force devotedly constructed by Marlborough sadly diminished in numbers and efficiency by the time the '15 Rebellion broke out, so that new regiments had to be hurriedly raised.

The long period of peace that followed under George I, accompanied as it was by constant Parliamentary attacks on the Army's existence, combined with maladministration and corruption, again ensured that the nation entered the War of the Austrian Succession in 1741 with inadequate and ill-prepared military forces. More regiments were raised and the great fighting qualities of the British soldier re-asserted themselves at Dettingen and Fontenoy. When, during the middle of a Continental campaign, the Army had to contend simultaneously with a serious rebellion in the home base in 1745, the deficiencies of the regiments at home were sadly displayed in Cope's shameful defeat at Prestonpans. Not until the battle-hardened regiments from Flanders were brought home by Cumberland, thus interrupting operations against France, was the rebellion crushed. The degree of initial success achieved by the three main Jacobite uprisings was therefore due in considerable measure to inept management of the Army by successive governments. The fact that the Army survived at all throughout this period was due, in Sir John Fortescue's opinion, to 'the spirit, the pride and the self-respect of individual regiments' which always had a number of officers 'who worked hard and conscientiously for the credit of their own corps'.

The regiments of the Army in the late 17th and early 18th centuries were divided into Horse, Dragoons and Foot, and, from 1716, the Royal Regiment of Artillery. The Horse consisted of big men on big steeds, whose chief rôle was to provide shock action by the controlled charge of mounted swordsmen. As they featured little in any of the Jacobite rebellions they will not be considered further.

In the 17th century, Dragoons were the handymen of the Army who, though mounted for greater mobility, were trained primarily to fight on foot. They were less numerous than the Horse. They were invaluable for the tasks of advance,

flank and rearguards, reconnaissance, outposts and escorts, and as such were far more useful in terrain like the Scottish Highlands than the cumbersome Horse or slow-moving Foot. During the War of the Spanish Succession their mounted infantry rôle tended to lapse and, since they were cheaper than Horse to raise and maintain, they became increasingly used as pure cavalry, the number of their regiments now surpassing those of the Horse; at the outbreak of the '15, for example, no less than 13 new dragoon regiments were raised. Nevertheless they could still be called upon to fight on foot, as was seen at Preston in 1715, when six of the seven regiments that attacked the Jacobites were dismounted dragoons. At Glenshiel in 1719, where the country was unsuitable for mounted action, the Scots Greys also attacked on foot. By the time of the '45, however, dragoons, though still armed with musket and bayonet as well as a sword, had become virtually indistinguishable from the Horse in employment. The regiments engaged in Scotland did not show to much advantage in set-piece battles, despite the Highlanders' dislike of cavalry, but did useful work in the advance to contact and pursuit.

The strength of a dragoon regiment fluctuated considerably according to the establishment in force at the time and other factors. In William III's time a regiment was supposed to be 480 strong, formed in eight troops, but the regiments employed in the '15 and '45 averaged little more than 200 each, providing two squadrons each of probably only two troops, in which the men were formed for battle in three, sometimes two, ranks.

Of the 34,000 troops in Britain that William III inherited, 25,000 were infantry, regiments of Guards (3) and of Foot. In the period 1689–1745 this number would vary, being more than doubled during the War of the Spanish Succession, but only totalling 33,000 out of an army of 40,000 in 1745. Up until 1760 each regiment of Foot was known by its colonel's name, its title therefore altering when it changed hands, although some had additional designations, like the Royal Regiment (later Royal Scots), which took precedence after the Foot Guards, or the Royal Regiment of Ireland. During the second quarter of the 18th

1 and 3. Highland clansmen, 1689
2. Highland chief, 1689

A

1. Musketeer, Hasting's Regt., 1689
2. Captain, Earl of Angus's Regt., 1689
3. Pikeman, Earl of Argyll's Regt., 1692

1. Musketeer, Spanish infantry, 1719
2. Highland chief, 1715
3. Trooper, Lowland Horse, 1715

C

1. Grenadier, Earl of Forfar's Regt., 1715
2 and 3. Officers, Montague's Regt., 1719

1. Colonel, Lord Ogilvy's Regt., 1745
2. Junior officer, clan regiment, 1745
3. Front rank man, clan regiment, 1745

1. Private, Independent Highland Coy., 1740
2. Fusilier, Régt. Royal-Écossais, 1746
3. Trooper, Baggot's Hussars, 1745
4. Sergeant, Irish Picquets, 1745

F

1. Grenadier, Ligonier's Regt., 1746
2. Gunner, Royal Artillery, 1746
3. Officers, Cobham's Dragoons, 1746

G

1. Drummer, Barrell's Regt., 1746
2. Officer, Royal North British Fusiliers, 1746
3. Corporal, Munro's Regt., 1746

H

century the precedence of regiments became fixed and recognised by numerals which first appeared in the 1742 Army List.

Unlike some Continental armies, the regiment had a single battalion, except in the Guards and the Royal Regiment which each had two. A battalion consisted of a headquarters staff and 13 companies, the strength of which would vary, according to the establishment in force at the time, from 30 to 60 men per company. Theoretically a battalion in wartime should have been some 800 all ranks, but many factors—failure to recruit, desertions, sickness, casualties and detachments—could reduce the strength considerably. Mackay's six battalions at Killiecrankie averaged 720 men each, but the average strength of the 15 battalions at Culloden was only 485: 22 officers, 22 sergeants, 15 drummers and 367 rank and file (corporals and privates).

One of the 13 companies was composed of grenadiers, a new type of infantryman introduced in about 1678. These were picked men, chosen for their height, strength and soldierly qualities, and as such were expected to set an example to the rest of the battalion, whether in a standing fire-fight or storming a breach. Besides his musket, bayonet and sword, the grenadier was equipped with three hand-grenades and a hatchet, although the latter was discontinued in the 18th century and the use of grenades was reserved for siege operations.

The remaining companies of a 17th-century regiment were composed of pikemen and musketeers. Before the introduction of grenadiers the élite of a battalion had been its pikemen, whose task was to protect the musketeers, whose cumbersome and slow-to-load firearms made them highly vulnerable to cavalry or enemy pikes. By the time of William III, largely due to an improvement in firearms and an increasing reliance on firepower, the proportion of pikemen to musketers in an infantry company had dropped to one in five. The invention of the bayonet further hastened the demise of the pikeman since it enabled the musketeer to defend himself at close quarters. But it was not until the adoption of the socket bayonet which, unlike the plug-in type that had been the downfall of so many of Mackay's infantry at Killiecrankie, permitted the musketeer

to fire his weapon with bayonet ready-fixed, that the pikeman's days were numbered, the pike being finally abolished in 1704.

Thus by the '15 and the '45 the bulk of the battalion was composed of ordinary musketeers armed with musket, bayonet and sword. The 17th-century matchlock, inaccurate, unreliable, its 44 movements for loading giving a rate of fire of only one round a minute, was gradually replaced towards the end of the century by the flintlock, more reliable and with double the rate of fire, though without much improvement in range and accuracy. In 1689 both matchlocks and flintlocks were in use, but William III's efforts to modernise his infantry's weapons led to the manufacture of an improved flintlock which developed, after 1715, into the famous 'Brown Bess' or Tower Musket, arguably the best infantry weapon in Europe. Its reliability and speed of loading were further enhanced around 1730 by the substitution of an iron ramrod instead of the wooden type.

A 17th-century battalion on the march would advance by companies, the grenadiers leading, each company having a frontage of between 6 and 20 files, depending on the road space available. When it formed line of battle, the pikemen of each company would usually be concentrated as one body in the centre of the line, so as to be able to form a square into which the musketeers could retire in the event of attack by cavalry. Until this occurred the musketeers would be deployed either side of the pikes, formed usually in five or six ranks. To fire, each rank would march forward a few paces, discharge their muskets, and then counter-march to the rear to reload. The grenadiers would be either split between each wing or deployed on the right flank.

Following the disappearance of the pikemen, and the experience gained in William's Low Countries campaign of the importance of infantry firepower as a battle-winning factor, the British Foot adopted the platoon firing system. For this the men would form in three ranks and the 12 battalion companies divided up into 16 equal-strength platoons, with two more provided by the grenadiers on either flank; if the battalion was at low strength, only 12 platoons would be told off, plus the grenadiers. The platoons were

A contemporary engraving of the different phases of the
Battle of Culloden, showing the Royal troops on the right
and the Jacobite army on the left. (National Army Museum)

then grouped into at least three 'firings', the
platoons forming each firing being staggered
along the battalion line, so that fire could be kept
up from all parts of it. Within the platoons the
front rank would kneel to fire, while the second
and third stood, the latter firing between the
files of the former. On the word of command, or
by drum-beat, the platoons of the first firing would
discharge a volley and then reload, while the next
firing took up the fusillade and so on. (For further
details and diagram, see Men-at-Arms 97, *Marlborough's Army.*)

This method of delivering a battalion's musketry proved so effective in the War of the Spanish
Succession that it continued in use for the next
30 years. However, whereas under Marlborough
the whole battalion halted before commencing
its fire, by the time of Fontenoy in 1745 battalions
were trained to continue their advance as they
fired. To effect this, the platoons of each firing
stepped out while the remainder stepped short.
The advanced firing halted and volleyed, by
which time the remainder had caught up, en-
abling the next firing to advance in its turn. By

this means a continuous fire and movement was
maintained.

The British infantry covered itself with glory
against the French at Dettingen and Fontenoy,
but it was fighting against opponents comparable
in weapons and organisation, if less well-trained.
In the '45 it faced a wild and savage onrush for
which, until after Falkirk, it had not been trained.
The regiments that broke at Prestonpans were
raw and inexperienced and under an incompetent
commander, Cope. However, some of those that
did the same at Falkirk were veterans of Fontenoy,
although their rout was largely due to the dila-
toriness of their hated commander, Hawley, and
his misguided contempt for the enemy, which
combined to place them at a tactical disadvantage
to the Jacobites. When Cumberland arrived in
Scotland he restored the troops' morale and
retrained them in how best to resist the Highland
charge. After previously thinning the enemy ranks
with gunfire and steady volleys, they broke the
actual impact with a *chevaux-de-frise* of bayonets,
in the same way that the pikemen of the previous
century had met the onset of charging cavalry.

The increasing use of light infantry in Continental armies for outpost, reconnaissance and
security duties was paralleled in the British service
by the formation, first of companies, then of

regiments, of Highlanders loyal to the Government. Further details of these can be found under Plate F1.

As stated earlier, the Royal Regiment of Artillery was formed in 1716. In William III's and Queen Anne's wars special trains of artillery had to be formed by the Board of Ordnance, but these were always reduced in peacetime. It was the disclosure of an almost total lack of any artillery arm when the '15 broke out that led to the formation of the Royal Artillery, but it remained quite separate administratively from the rest of the Army under the Ordnance Board. By 1745 the Regiment had ten companies and a cadet-company. A company usually had seven officers, 14 NCOs, two drummers, 20 gunners and 64 matrosses (gunners' assistants). At Glenshiel in 1719 Wightman had a detachment of four 'Cohoorns', a light-weight mortar discharging a grenade; but artillery played no significant rôle in the Rebellions until Culloden, where Captain Cunningham's Company made a major contribution to Cumberland's victory. The company disposed of ten brass 3-pdrs. which were sited in pairs in the intervals between the battalions of the first line, and five howitzers between the first

and second line. Both types of gun did great execution on the Jacobites before they charged, with the 3-pdrs. changing to case-shot to supplement the infantry's musketry when the clans came on.

The usual range for a 3-pdr. firing round shot was about 400–500 yards, though greater ranges could be achieved by elevating the barrel; case shot was only effective at ranges up to 200 yards. The range of a howitzer firing explosive shell was about 1,300 yards. A 3-pdr. could be manned by a crew of six and an NCO, two guns forming a detachment under an officer, while the howitzer required a crew of five.

So seriously was the threat of the '45 taken in England that some of the County Militia, a gravely neglected and almost useless force, were called out, and numbers of the nobility undertook to raise 12 regiments of foot and two of horse at their own expense, for service in any part of the

'Rebell Gratitude'. The shooting of Captain Grosett, Engineer and ADC to Cumberland, by a Highland officer whose life had been spared. The Jacobite is about to be cut down by the infantrymen with their hangers. Note the corporal's shoulder knot on the left-hand figure. A contemporary engraving. (National Galleries of Scotland)

A painting by William Delacour representing Sir Stuart Threipland of Fingask as a Jacobite fugitive after Culloden. The very voluminous belted plaid, waistcoat and jacket all have a green ground, dark and light red, bright green and brown stripes, but the plaid is of a different pattern to the other garments. The bonnet is blue. (Mr and Mrs Mark Murray Threipland, Fingask Castle, Perth)

Kingdom while the emergency lasted. One of the latter, Kingston's Light Horse, gave good service in the latter part of the Rebellion and fought at Culloden. On its formal disbandment in September 1746 it was promptly reraised as a regular regiment, the Duke of Cumberland's Dragoons, serving in Flanders until 1748.

In addition to these semi-regular regiments, a number of volunteer units were raised for local defence, which included such exotically named corps as General Oglethorpe's Royal Foxhunters, the Yorkshire Blues, the Loyal Blue Fusiliers and the Loyal Associators. Despite all these accretions to the regular forces, the Government also thought it necessary to acquire on a mercenary basis 6,000 Hessian troops, who performed garrison duties in Perthshire and Stirlingshire in March 1746.

Finally, it must not be forgotten how much the foiling of the Stuarts' hopes of regaining their throne was due to the Royal Navy. Whether in action against French fleets, as in 1692 and 1708, maintaining the constant watch and ward over French invasion ports, ship-to-shore action as in

1719, or patrolling the Scottish coast and islands, it was the Navy that ensured the non-arrival of French troops, arms and supplies on which the Jacobite uprisings depended so greatly for success. Only twice could the Navy be said to have failed: it could not stop the Young Pretender reaching Scotland in 1745 and was unable to prevent his escape to France the following year.

Regiments engaged in the chief actions of the Rebellions, 1689–1746

Since the colonel's name, by which regiments were known throughout this period, changed frequently, they are shown below by their more familiar numbers, except in the case of a regiment disbanded after a campaign.

Abbreviations: * = Scots regiment. † = Scots-Dutch. + = Dutch. K = Killiecrankie. D = Dunkeld. G = Glencoe. Pn = Preston. S = Sherriffmuir. P = Prestonpans. F = Falkirk. C = Culloden.

Uniform: All coats red, except Dutch (+) and Royal Artillery (blue). Facings where known abbreviated as follows: bl = blue. bf = buff. gn = green. gy = grey. r = red. w = white. y = yellow. ? = uncertain.

1689	1715	1719	1745
Dragoons	*Horse*	*Dragoons*	*Dragoons*
Annandale's.* K.	3rd (Bays) Pn. bf.	2nd.* bl.	10th. F, C. y.
Belhaven's.* K.	*Dragoons*	*Foot*	11th. C. w.
Foot	2nd.* S. bl.	11th. gn?	13th. P, F. gn.
13th. K. y.	3rd. S. bl?	14th. y?	14th. P, F. y.
25th.* K. y.	4th. S. gn.	15th. y.	Kingston's. C. gn.
26th.* D. w.	6th. S. y?	Huffel's.+	*RA*
Kenmure's.* K.	7th. S. w?	Amerongen's.+	Cunningham's. C. r.
Mackay's.† K. r.	9th. Pn. bf.	Highland Coys.*	*Foot*
Balfour's.† K.	11th. Pn. bf.		1st.* F, C. bl.
Ramsay's.† K. w.	13th. Pn. y/gn.		3rd. F, C. bf.
Argyll's.* G. y.	14th. Pn. y.		4th. F, C. bl.
	Stanhope's. Pn.		6th. P. y.
	Foot		8th. F, C. bl.
	3rd. S. bf		13th. F, C. y.
	8th. S. y.		14th, F, C. bf.
	11th. S. gn?		20th. C. y.
	14th. S. y?		21st.* C. bl.
	17th. S. gy?		25th.* C. y.
	21st.* S. bl.		27th. F, C. bf.
	25th.* S. y.		34th. F, C. y.
	26th.* Pn. y.		36th. F, C. gn.
	36th. S. gn.		37th. F, C. y.
			44th. P. y.
			46th. P. y.
			47th. P. w.
			48th. F, C. bf.
			Battereau's. F, C. y.
			Loudon's (part)* P, F, C. w. or bf.
			Argyll Militia.* F, C.

Note The Foot regiments, 44th, 46th, 47th and 48th, were numbered in 1745 as 45th, 47th, 48th and 49th but are shown here under the numbers they bore from 1748 to 1881.

Uniforms

Jacobite Forces

Uniform as such was unknown in Jacobite armies except for the foreign contingents and the Prince's Life Guards in 1745, whose 'cloathing was blue faced with red' and 'scarlat thrums bonnets'. Uniformity of a sort was achieved by the wearing of Highland dress, or at least elements of it, by clan and non-clan regiments alike. One of the first measures during the formation of the Earl of Cromarty's regiment, raised partially in the lowlands of north-east Scotland, was 'the making of Highland clothes'. Even the unfortunate Manchester regiment had tartan sashes.

During the 50-odd years of the Rebellions the basic dress of the Highlander was the belted plaid, a rectangle of tartan cloth about six yards by two, which was belted round the waist so that the lower portion hung to the knees as a roughly pleated skirt, leaving the mass of material either to be wrapped round the upper part of the body, or draped up and fastened near the left shoulder to leave the arms free. To this, according to his means, the Highlander would add a woollen bonnet, a shirt, waistcoat, jacket or short coat, hose and shoes. A feature of Highland upper garments in the 17th and early 18th centuries was the slashing of sleeves and breasts of the coat. Alternatively, and sometimes additionally, he might wear close-fitting trousers, or trews, a garb more usually favoured by the upper classes out of doors, since it was more convenient for riding. From around 1725 some Highlanders began to wear the 'little kilt', which was simply the plaid with the upper and more voluminous portion cut off. This was the forerunner of the modern kilt, though it must be remembered that Highland dress was banned for nearly 40 years after the '45, except in Highland regiments, and did not regain its popularity until after 1822, by which time it was very different from that worn before proscription.

There is not space here to enter into the complex question of tartan cloth and its various setts, for which recourse must be made to the numerous books on the subject (see 'Recommended Further Reading'). It is enough to say that the notion of a particular clan being distinguished by its own sett did not apply during the Rebellions. Members of a clan recognised each other by the badge in their bonnets. In the 18th century the only

Two Jacobite prisoners escorted by four infantryment. Note the soldiers' knapsacks. Their coat skirts are not turned back, nor are they wearing marching gaiters, as was more usual. Water-colour by Paul Sandby, who accompanied Cumberland's army. (British Museum)

Camp of Royal troops at Fort Augustus after its siege by the Jacobites. Loch Ness lies beyond. Note the heavy gun in the foreground and the soldiers playing some form of bowls. Water-colour by Thomas Sandby. (Reproduced by gracious permission of H.M. The Queen.)

uniformity of sets was to be found in the Government's Highland regiments, and the clan tartans of today originate from no earlier than the 19th century; as indeed do such items as large and highly decorative sporrans or purses, ornate plaid brooches and 'sgian dubhs' stuck in the hose-tops. The earlier Highlander's purse was a small leather pouch suspended from his waistbelt, while he fastened up his plaid either with a bodkin or a loop and button.

Government Forces

The basic clothing for a soldier throughout this period consisted of a broad-brimmed hat, or cap for grenadiers, shirt and neckcloth, waistcoat, knee-length coat, breeches, stockings, shoes, or long boots for mounted men. Apart from the Royal Artillery and a few of William III's regiments, which were clothed in blue, red was the universal colour for coats and most waistcoats. In the 17th century breeches might be of a different colour, but by the 18th all were red, or blue for Royal regiments. Initially stockings were sometimes coloured but eventually all were white. The coats were lined and faced in contrasting colours according to the colonel's preference. The cut of the clothing generally followed civilian fashions, but gradually a specific military style emerged. The practice of embellishing the coats with lengths of tape or lace, originally white or yellow but later in coloured patterns, was at first confined to grenadiers and drummers but in time became a regimental distinguishing feature of all coats.

Regimental colonels were allowed considerable, though not complete, latitude over their men's clothing, and choice of insignia to adorn the grenadier caps and drums. It was not until the accession of George II that the style, facing colours, regimental lace patterns and distinctive badges began to be regularised, culminating in the publication in 1742 of the important document 'A Representation of the Cloathing of His Majesty's Household and all forces upon the Establishments of Great Britain and Ireland', which illustrated the dress of every regiment.

Officers' dress was not regulated. Apart from wearing red, conforming to their colonel's requirements if any were specified, and displaying the symbols of commissioned rank—the sash and gorget—when on duty, they were permitted considerable freedom of choice in the embellishment or otherwise of their clothing. Even the adoption of the regimental facing colour was by no means compulsory. However, under the influence of the Hanoverian monarchs a higher standard of uniformity and conformity with the men's dress was gradually achieved.

The development of accoutrements over the period can be seen in the Plates and notes thereto, which follow; these also include comments on personal weapons of officers and men, additional to those in the earlier section, on Government forces.

The Plates

A1: *Highland Clansman, 1689*

At the lowest social level of the Highland clan stood the common 'humbly'. In the battle line such men formed the rear ranks, armed perhaps with no more than a club, an agricultural implement or, as shown here, a Lochaber axe. Because of his poverty, his clothing may have consisted solely of a belted plaid and bonnet; he may have gone barefoot or possessed a pair of deer-hide 'cuarans'. The plaid on this figure, which is worn pulled up over the shoulders as was done in inclement weather, is of undyed wool with a few simple stripes of blue, a favourite colour among Highlanders, and brown, for which a bark-dye was used.

A2: *Highland Chief, 1689*

At the other end of the social scale was the clan chief. The clothing of this figure is based on a description of Alasdair MacDonald, otherwise known as MacIain of Glencoe, at the gathering of the clans under Dundee in 1689. In his bonnet he wears the heather badge of Clan Donald. Beneath a buff leather coat, perhaps a relic of the Civil War, is a green doublet. Trews are worn, and if he had a plaid with him it would be arranged as in B3 or E1. Under his doublet he wears a waist belt to which are attached his dirk, sporran and pistol. His targe is slung on his back; a bandolier suspends the powder charges and priming flask, and his broadsword is slung from a shoulder belt.

A3: *Highland Clansman, 1689*

This figure represents the main fighting strength of the clan, a swordsman of the type that broke Mackay's infantry at Killiecrankie. Having discarded his plaid, as was the custom, he stands ready for the onset, in jacket and shirt, the latter perhaps secured between his thighs with the bodkin used to fasten the loose end of his plaid at his left shoulder. Note the short jacket with its slashed sleeves. His plaid is predominantly black, another fairly common colour for early tartans, with yellow lines. In his bonnet is the holly badge

Dragoon of Lord Mark Kerr's, or 11th Regiment of Dragoons. *Coat:* **red, white cuffs, buff lining.** *Waistcoat:* **white.** *Breeches:* **red.** *Cloak* **(rolled behind saddle): red, lined buff.** *Flask cord* **on pouch belt: buff.** *Horse furniture:* **buff with red, black or blue embroidery. From the 1742 Clothing Book. (National Army Museum)**

of Clan Maclean, who formed the right wing and part of the left at Killiecrankie.

B1: *Musketeer, Hastings's Regiment of Foot, 1689*

Hastings's (later 13th Foot) was the only English regiment at Killiecrankie, and with Leven's (25th Foot) formed the only part of Mackay's force that was not broken by the Highland charge. The clothing shown comes from an Inspection Report of 1686 (although this shows grey stockings). Accoutrements consist of the bandolier, with its individual wooden or leather powder charges, bullet bag and priming flask, soon to be replaced by the 'cartouch box'; and a waist belt to carry the sword and plug bayonet. The musket could not be fired with this bayonet fixed, and the defeat at Killiecrankie was said to have been hastened by the clans falling on the Government line before the musketeers could fix bayonets.

B2: *Captain, Earl of Angus's Regiment of Foot, 1689*

Although Dundee's Highlanders overcame almost twice their number at Killiecrankie with com-

Battalion company man of Ligonier's, later Conway's Regiment, 48th Foot. From the 1742 Clothing Book. See Plate G1 for grenadier and colours of uniform. (National Army Museum)

B3: Pikeman, Earl of Argyll's Regiment of Foot, 1692
This, one of the first Highland regiments to be raised, was formed in 1689, largely from the Earl of Argyll's Clan Campbell with Lowland Scots NCOs. Except for the blue bonnets bearing Argyll's coronet and boar's-head crest, it was dressed the same as the English Army. Pikemen had by now discarded the helmets and armour worn some years previously and were dressed similarly to the musketeers. They were armed with a sword and 16ft. pike. The costume is based on research by John Prebble for his book *Glencoe* among original documents at Inverary Castle dealing with the raising of the regiment. Apparently the men were issued with 'green plaids' to withstand the Highland winter, but the details of the sett are not known. The regiment was disbanded in 1698 after fighting with great bravery in the Low Countries, thus redeeming its reputation after the notoriety it had gained for its part in the Massacre of Glencoe.

C1: Musketeer, Spanish Infantry, 1719
Some 5,000 Spanish troops were sent to assist the rising in 1719 but, owing to storms at sea, only 300 arrived in Scotland to stand with the Highland army at Glenshiel. This infantryman wears the red cockade of Spain to which the Jacobite white may have been added. His coat and breeches are of undyed wool, a cloth in common use with several European armies, regiments being distinguished by different facing colours. His cartouch box is on his waistbelt in front and a priming flask is slung over the left shoulder. His short sword, or hanger, and bayonet are suspended from a frog attached to the waist belt. Despite being isolated in a strange and inhospitable country, with allies who must have appeared wild and incomprehensible, the Spaniards put up a stout resistance at Glenshiel and fought on after the Highlanders had been routed, only surrendering the next day when further fighting was hopeless.

C2: Highland Chief, 1715
Although a chief or gentleman would normally wear trews, he would also adopt the belted plaid on occasions, as worn here. In his bonnet is the white cockade worn by Jacobites to distinguish

parative ease, they were routed three weeks later by the single regiment holding Dunkeld. This had been raised only four months before by the Earl of Angus from a stern sect of Lowland Covenanters known as Cameronians, a name adopted by the new regiment (later 26th Foot). Because of the latitude allowed to officers in their dress, the costume shown here is speculative. In view of the strongly Puritan nature of the regiment, it lacks much of the gold or silver lace which decorated officers' coats in considerable profusion in other corps. Commissioned rank is denoted by the waist sash, the gorget—gilt for captains, black with gilt studs for lieutenants, and silver for ensigns—and the half-pike. Although the men's coats are believed to have been faced white, most officers at this period and for several years to come did not wear the regimental facing colour. A reconstruction of a musketeer of Angus's appears in the mono illustrations.

themselves from Highlanders loyal to the Government, who wore the black cockade of Hanover. His blue doublet is slashed on the chest, sleeves and skirt in the Highland fashion; it is based on a portrait dated 1708 and was probably becoming somewhat old-fashioned by this date. The waist belt, which holds up the belted plaid and also suspends the dirk, sporran and pistol, is worn under the doublet. The pistol had a side-bar on the opposite side to the lock which clipped over the belt. The sword belt hangs from the right shoulder and a narrower strap over the right, with pickers for the pistol, supports a priming flask. Though his garb is entirely Highland he wears the full-bottomed wig of the English or Lowland Scots gentleman. The sett depicted is based on an actual piece of old tartan. The clansmen in the '15 would have differed little from A1 and A3.

C3: Trooper, Lowland Horse, 1715

This figure represents the cavalry troops raised by Lowland noblemen from eastern and south-west Scotland. He has a blue bonnet with white cockade, a common headgear all over Scotland. His short coat and waistcoat are based on surviving civilian garments of the period. Many troopers were without proper boots and rode in shoes and stockings, but this man has acquired a pair of dragoon boots and breeches, perhaps relics of service with the Royal Scots Dragoons (Greys) in Marlborough's campaigns. He is armed with a broadsword, a weapon found all over Scotland. Some of the Lowland cavalry had 'strong, hardy horses fit for the charge', but the English Jacobites were mounted on 'fleet blood horses, better adapted for the race-course and hunting field'.

D1: Grenadier, Earl of Forfar's Regiment of Foot, 1715

This regiment—better known as the Buffs (3rd Foot)—formed part of Argyll's army at Sherriffmuir. The uniform is taken from supporters on a memorial tablet to Sir Charles Wills, who succeeded Forfar as colonel in 1716, but with the latter's coronet and crest of a salamander in flames on the cap instead of the Wills crest shown on the tablet. The coat is now fuller in the skirt than in William III's time but otherwise the costume

Fusilier, Campbell's or Royal North British Fusiliers, 21st Foot. *Coat*: red, faced and lined blue. *Waistcoat*: red. *Breeches*: blue. *Lace*: blue zig-zag, yellow line. *Cap*: blue front with St Andrew's cross and star in white and green, red scrolls; little flap, blue, white border edged red with 'Royal Fuzileers' in red, thistle in full colour within. From the 1742 Clothing Book. See Plate H2 for officer. (National Army Museum)

has changed little, if at all, since Marlborough's day (see, once more, the author's '*Marlborough's Army 1702–11*', MAA 97). The white lace was, as a rule at this date, worn on the coats of grenadier companies only. The white marching gaiters had been introduced by Marlborough in 1710. The hats of battalion company men were now turned up on three sides. Grenadiers' pouches were larger than those of 'hat men' at this date, since they incorporated divisions for both cartridges and grenades. The musket sling, also, was issued to grenadiers only, so that they could sling the weapon when throwing grenades. The bayonet (now of the socket type fitting over the muzzle) and the hanger still had separate frogs.

D2, D3: Officers, Montague's Regiment of Foot, 1719

There is very little evidence of the dress of officers of George I's army; no regulations governed their costume, which was, of course, privately purchased, and which still followed civilian styles. D2 is based on a contemporary portrait, but is speculative for this particular regiment (later, 11th Foot), which formed part of Wightman's force at Glenshiel. The plain coat, with its lack of decorative lace, suggests a garment kept for field use and less formal occasions. The waistcoat, shorter than in the late 17th century, is still edged with gold lace, however. Commissioned rank is indicated by the gorget and the sash, the latter now more usually worn over the shoulder than around the waist. The sword belt is worn over the waistcoat but under the coat; as time passed and it became more common for the coat to be worn open for all duty, the sword belt was increasingly worn underneath the waistcoat as well. The use of a fusil in place of the spontoon (see H2) carried by battalion company officers since 1710 suggests a grenadier officer. Officers of these companies had caps like those of their men, but seem to have preserved them for ceremonial occasions, probably to spare their expensive embroidery. D3 shows an officer in a more decorative version of this basic uniform, probably typical of peacetime daily dress, showing the richer appointments of hat, waistcoat, coat, belt

Back and side view of an infantryman, c. 1745, showing a battalion man of the 1st Foot Guards. From 'The Gentleman Volunteer's Pocket Companion describing the Manual Exercise'. Note the hair tied back with a ribbon on the left-hand figure; the end of the queue appears to be tucked under the coat collar. (National Army Museum)

and garters. Note that the lacing did not indicate rank at this date, merely officer status and—probably—personal means.

E1: Colonel, Lord Ogilvy's or Angus Regiment, 1745
This non-clan regiment, raised in Angus, joined the Jacobite army at Edinburgh in October 1745; it eventually had two battalions. The costume depicted here of jacket, trews and plaid is based on a portrait of Lord Ogilvy. Clothing in these small checks can be found in a number of portraits of the period. Although the plaid is the same colour as the jacket and trews, it is of a different sett. Despite this not being a Highland corps the full complement of Highland weapons is carried. When the regiment arrived at Edinburgh Ogilvy ordered all his officers to equip themselves with targes, 2,000 of which had to be provided by the city armourers, presumably for the men of the non-clan regiments.

E2: Junior officer, clan regiment, 1745
Although this officer wears the yew badge of Clan Fraser behind the white cockade in his bonnet, he may be considered fairly typical of any of the clan regiments. The varied tartans on this figure and E3 are based on those shown by Morier in his painting of Culloden, contemporary evidence which refutes the theory of clan tartans. The belted plaid was still in common use, but this officer wears the 'philabeg' or little kilt. Besides the broadsword and dirk he carries two pistols, one clipped to a shoulder strap, the other to the dirk belt worn over the waistcoat. The sporran hangs from the belt which supports the kilt; the targe is slung over the left shoulder.

E3: Front rank man, clan regiment, 1745
The superior and well-equipped men chosen for the foremost ranks would have had muskets and one or more of the traditional Highland weapons. This clansman has a priming flask slung over his left shoulder and carries the cartridges for his musket—which averaged only 12 per man—in his sporran. The belt, which supported the sporran and dirk and held up the belted plaid, is worn under the waistcoat. The foresight of Lord George Murray ensured that some, if not all the regiments had haversacks and canteens for use on the march.

F1: Private, Independent Highland Company, c. 1740
Independent companies of Government High-landers to keep the peace in the turbulent glens had first been raised in 1667, but were disbanded in 1717. After the 1719 rising it was decided that the internal security of the area required a permanent force of constabulary, and in 1725 the companies were revived, chiefly from Clans Campbell, Grant and Munro. In 1739 a number of companies were grouped together to form the Highland Regiment, better known as the Black Watch. To counter the '45 Rebellion another Highland regiment was raised by Lord Loudon, as well as an additional 18 independent companies.

Before 1717 the companies had all worn their own Highland dress, but it would appear that those formed in 1725 were given short red jackets and waistcoats to wear over the belted plaid to distinguish them as Government troops. Unlike the Jacobite clan regiments, these units also sought uniformity in the plaids, which were ordered to be of 'the same Sort and Colour'. From this ruling there emerged in due course the sett known as the Government tartan. Initially this probably differed in detail according to the company's area of recruitment, but the basic colours of blue, black and green came to be worn by both the Highland regiments and the independent companies.

There is no pictorial evidence of the companies' dress before 1740, but it was doubtless similar to that shown for the Highland Regiment in the early 1740s. The bonnet had a red ribbon threaded through the brow band, to ensure a close fit: it probably bore the black cockade to which was added, by Government Highlanders in the '45, a red saltire cross. The jacket was cut in Highland fashion to accommodate the belted plaid, the upper part of which can be seen looped up to a button behind the left shoulder. The jackets of both Highland regiments were lined and faced buff, though whether this also applied to the independent companies is uncertain. Each man had, besides his musket and bayonet, a full complement of Highland weapons: broadsword slung from a shoulder belt, pistol clipped to a narrower belt over the same shoulder and passing under the left armpit, and dirk suspended beside

Private, the Duke of Cumberland's Dragoons, 1746, formerly Kingston's Light Horse which was raised for the '45. Coat: red, faced and lined green, brass buttons, yellow braid loops, yellow aiguillette. Waistcoat, breeches and gloves: buff. Hat lace gold, sprig of leaves behind the cockade. Accoutrements: buff. Cloak: red, lined green. Horse furniture: green, yellow embroidery. Painting by David Morier. (Reproduced by gracious permission of H.M. The Queen)

the sporran on the waist belt, which also supported a buff leather cartouch box. Targes seem to have been optional.

F2: Fusilier, Régiment Royal-Écossais, 1746
Apart from individual officers the only regular troops sent by France to aid the Rebellion were the Franco-Irish Fitzjames's Horse (red coats faced blue—see MAA 102, *The Wild Geese*), and Lord John Drummond's 'Royal-Écossais', plus detachments of Franco-Irish foot regiments. Due to the vigilance of the Royal Navy only one squadron of Fitzjames's reached Scotland to fight at Culloden, with 300 of the 'Royal-Écossais'. The majority of the French infantry of the day had uniforms of greyish-white, coloured coats being reserved for the foreign regiments. The weapons and accoutrements are of the normal French infantry pattern. Note the priming flask beneath the cartouch box; and, on the smaller view, the arrangement of pocket buttons and a typical knapsack.

An officer (left), private and sergeant of Government Highlanders. See Plate D3. (National Army Museum)

F3: Trooper, Baggot's Hussars, 1745
Command of a small body of Jacobite horse raised in Edinburgh in October 1745 was given to a Franco-Irish officer in the French service, the troop then being named after him as Baggot's Hussars—a type of cavalry which had existed in the French service for half a century. No precise description of their appearance—which, like that of most of the Jacobites, was probably diverse—survives; but two separate non-Jacobite accounts mention such items as 'large Fur-Caps', 'close Plaid-Waistcoats' and 'limber [supple] boots'. It seems possible that Baggot would have modelled the fur caps—not a Scottish headdress—on those of the French hussars; and since the short Highland coat was of similar length to the normal waistcoat of the day, it was probably the former that the eyewitness saw. As to arms, one account mentions 'long swords or shabbers [sabres]'; while another speaks of 'a brace [of pistols] in the girdles, a broad sword, and a musket slung on his shoulder'. This trooper carries twin pistols

on his saddle, a broadsword, and a musket, with a priming flask and shot pouch attached, slung over his shoulder.

F4: Sergeant, Irish Picquets (Régiment Dillon), 1745
It had been intended to send to Scotland 50 men from each of the six Franco-Irish regiments—Dillon's, Ruth's, Lally's, Clare's, Bulkeley's and Berwick's; but in the event only the detachments of the first three were able to join the Prince's army, in which they formed a weak battalion known as the Irish Picquets. At Culloden it was placed on the left flank of the second Jacobite line. All these regiments wore red coats with different facings, Dillon's being black with white metal buttons, Ruth's blue with blue waistcoats and breeches and brass buttons, and Lally's green with green waistcoats and brass buttons. The rank and file had the same weapons and accoutrements as F2; this sergeant's rank is marked by the band of silver lace round the cuff, and the 'halbert' which he carries in addition to his sword.

G1: Grenadier, Ligonier's Regiment of Foot, 1746
This regiment, one of those despatched from

Flanders to Scotland, was raised in 1742 as the 49th Foot but became the 48th in 1748; its colonel changed during the Rebellion, and by Culloden it was known as Conway's. The costume shown is based on an actual cap in the National Army Museum, and the 1742 Clothing Book, but with the grey marching gaiters issued in Flanders substituted for the white type. Unlike D1, this grenadier now has two pouches, the large one for grenades being slung over the left shoulder and a smaller cartouch box being worn on a waist belt at the front. The hanger and bayonet are now worn in a combined frog. On the march knapsacks were carried, usually made of animal hide and slung over one shoulder. A battalion company man of this regiment appears in the monochrome illustrations. Ligonier's distinguished itself at Falkirk, being the only regiment besides Barrell's which did not break under the Highland charge— unlike Ligonier's other regiment, the 13th Dragoons, which fled as soon as the Jacobites opened fire. As Conway's at Culloden it was placed to the left of the second line.

G2: Gunner, Royal Artillery, 1746

The Royal Regiment of Artillery was the only corps of the Army other than the Royal Horse Guards not clothed in red. Apart from officers and NCOs, the men were divided into gunners, equipped with a linstock or field staff and a powder horn for priming, and matrosses, or gunners' assistants, who carried muskets and bayonets. NCOs were armed with halberts, and swords like the gunners'. Officers carried a sword and a fusil, for which they wore a white cartouch box at the front of the waist belt supporting the sword. The officers' coats were also blue with red cuffs and linings, but with blue lapels; their breeches and waistcoats were red, and they wore a crimson sash over the left shoulder.

G3: Officers, Cobham's Regiment of Dragoons, 1746

Cobham's, or the 10th Dragoons, were raised in 1715; the regiment fought at Falkirk and Culloden. The costume shown is based on the description of a portrait of an officer, c. 1741; we have given the left-hand figure a 'boat cloak' typical of the type of protection worn by officers of the day on campaign. The NCOs and dragoons had yellow facings, waistcoats and breeches, but this officer's dress follows the earlier practice of not conforming to the men's; he has scarlet cuffs and breeches, silver lace loops, and a buff waistcoat. His rank is indicated by the sash over the left shoulder, the silver knot at the right shoulder, and the silver knot and tassel on the holster caps. The men's housings and holster caps were yellow, bearing on the latter the design of a knight's helm above trophies of colours, drums, trumpets and arms embroidered in red and black (or dark blue). Officers were armed with a sword and two pistols; dragoons with a musket and bayonet, two pistols, and a basket-hilted sword. They were accoutred with a pouch belt with a buff flask-cord in the centre, and a waist belt with a frog—see monochrome illustration of the 11th Dragoons.

Grenadier officer's cap of the Cumberland Militia, embodied during the '45. Front and turn-up behind blue, edged silver lace; front embroidered with Lowther arms, crest and cypher in silver, the hand on the white shield being red. The flap in front, red with a gold grenade and silver embroidery. Bag at back, red with silver and crimson tuft at top, silver embroidery. (Photo: G. A. Embleton)

H1: Drummer, Barrell's or King's Own Regiment of Foot, 1746

Barrell's (4th Foot) held its ground at Falkirk, and bore the brunt of the Jacobite attack on Cumberland's left at Culloden. It was known colloquially as the 'Old Tangereers', having been raised in 1680 for service at Tangier. This drummer's costume is based on that shown in Morier's Culloden painting. Since it was a Royal regiment he wears a red coat faced blue, with a special lace differing slightly from the blue zig-zag worn by the rest of the regiment. His belts and drum sling are covered with the same lace. Drummers of non-Royal regiments wore coats of the facing colour, faced red. All drummers wore caps resembling those of grenadiers but lower in height, and with special badges. A curious feature of drummers' coats of this period was the false sleeves hanging from the shoulders down the back. They were armed with a hanger suspended by a frog from the waist belt. In battle the two drummers of each company performed important tasks, maintaining the step as the battalion advanced, and relaying their captain's orders by drumbeat. The fife had been popular as an accompaniment to the drum in the 17th century, but had been discontinued in infantry regiments until re-introduced in 1748. Dragoon regiments had drums like the infantry, and one hautbois per troop.

H2: Officer, Campbell's or Royal North British Fusiliers, 1746

Although the official title of this regiment (21st Foot) had changed after the Act of Union, it was still commonly known by the earlier 'Scotch' or 'Scots Fuzileers'. This uniform is based on a portrait by Allan Ramsay of Major Hon. Andrew Sandilands. All ranks of Fusilier regiments wore

The stages of putting on the large plaid. (G. A. Embleton)

© G.A.EMBLETON

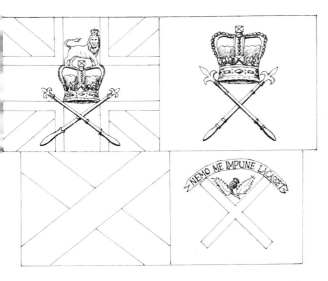

Top: Colours of Barrell's or King's Own Regiment of Foot. Right: Colonel's Colour, gold crown and sceptres on blue ground. Left: Lieutenant-Colonel's Colour, gold Royal Crest, crown and sceptres on Union flag (England and Scotland only). These Colours were carried at Culloden. (Scale: hoist of top left Colour = 6 feet.) Bottom: Jacobite Regimental Colours. Right: 2nd Battalion, Lord Ogilvy's Regiment, white St Andrew's Cross, thistle in natural colours, black and gold motto on white scroll, all on light blue ground. Left: Stuart of Appin's Regiment, yellow St Andrew's Cross on light blue ground. Both were at Culloden.

shown, based on the 1742 Clothing Book, is typical of the mass of the British infantry of the period. Although the coat skirts were usually turned back for ease of movement here they hang naturally, as depicted in many contemporary pictures of the Rebellion, perhaps to protect the legs from the Highland weather. He is armed with musket, bayonet and hanger; cartridges are carried in the buff pouch suspended over the left shoulder on a broad belt, at the end of which is a brush and picker for cleaning out the musket lock. When going into action it was customary to leave all knapsacks and other impedimenta with the regimental baggage. Corporal's rank was indicated by a white shoulder knot. Sergeants wore a crimson waist sash with a stripe in the facing colour, and carried a halbert instead of a musket (see the grenadier sergeant in Morier's painting of Culloden). Just distinguishable here is the yellow worm in the regimental coat lace.

caps similar to the grenadiers', though slightly lower, but their officers seem to have worn hats in the field and kept their richly-embroidered caps for ceremonial. The buff waistcoat is another example of officers' dress not conforming with the men's, whose waistcoats were red. He carries a spontoon and sword, the latter suspended from a waist belt worn under the waistcoat. The gorget, in silver to match the coat lace, denotes that he is on duty, and the sash is worn over the opposite shoulder to officers of cavalry and artillery. A fusilier of this regiment can be found in the monochrome illustrations. Campbell's were sent to Scotland from the Flanders army, having fought at Dettingen in 1743 and Fontenoy in 1745; they were in the left centre of the first line at Culloden.

H3: Corporal, Munro's Regiment of Foot, 1746
Munro's, numbered the 37th Foot, also came from Flanders; it fought without distinction at Falkirk. It became Dejean's just before Culloden, where it redeemed itself by stubborn fighting alongside Barrell's on the left of the first line. The uniform

Recommended Further Reading:

The following books should be obtainable:
Baynes, John, *The Jacobite Rising of 1715* (1970)
Buchan, John, *The Massacre of Glencoe* (1933)
Chandler, David, *The Art of Warfare in the Age of Marlborough* (1976) [Covers period 1688–1748]
Daiches, David, *Charles Edward Stuart* (1973), (paperback 1975)
Forster, Margaret, *The Rash Adventurer. The Rise and Fall of Charles Edward Stuart* (1973)
Kemp, Hilary, *The Jacobite Rebellion* (1975) [Covers the '15 and '45]
Kinross, John, *Discovering Battlefields in Scotland* (1976)
Linklater, Eric, *The Prince in the Heather* (1965) (paperback 1976)
Prebble, John, *Glencoe* (1966) (paperback 1968)
Prebble, John, *Culloden* (1961) (paperback 1967)
Selby, John, *Over the Sea to Skye* (1973)
Sinclair-Stevenson, Christopher, *Inglorious Rebellion. The Jacobite Rising of 1708, 1715 and 1719* (1971)
Thomasson, K., and Buist, F., *Battles of the '45* (1962)
Costume:
Dunbar, J. Telfer, *History of Highland Dress* (1962)
Grange, R. M. D., *A Short History of the Scottish Dress* (1966)
Lawson, C. C. P., *A History of the Uniforms of the British Army*. Vol. I (1940), Vol. II (1941)

Glossary

References to the plates include their extended captions, see pages 31 to 39.

baldrick A belt or sling, worn over one shoulder to support a sword's scabbard. (p.12)

bandolier A shoulder belt for carrying ammunition. (plate B1)

broadsword Smaller weapon adopted in pace of the claymore. (p.18)

clan A group owing feudal loyalty to their chief. (p.17)

claymore "Claidheamh mor", a large, two-handed sword. (p.18)

dirk A dagger. (p.18)

Dragoons Troops who fight on foot but march mounted. (p.24)

fusil A light flint-lock musket carried by officers. (plate D3)

gorget Part of an officer's uniform, a metal plate hung from the neck. (plate B2)

humbly The lowest ranking class of Highlander. (plate A1)

Lochaber axe A blade mounted on a pole. (p.18, plate A1)

philabeg The little kilt, a tartan skirt-like garment. (p.29, plate E2)

plaid A large (6 feet by 18 feet or 1.8 metre by 5.5 metre) piece of tartan cloth used as a garment, the belted plaid. (p.12, 29, 38 and plates C2 and F1)

sett The precise pattern of a tartan. (p.29)

spontoon A half-pike, a short spear carried by an officer. (plates B2 and H2)

targe A round shield. (p.13, 18, plate A3)

trews Close-fitting trousers. (p.29, plate E1)

Index

Figures in **bold** refer to illustrations

Places to visit

North-west Scotland

The Battle of Glenshiel, 10 June 1719
Location: About five miles south-east of Shiel Bridge where the A87 crosses the River Shiel. A nearby cairn marks the old bridge. National Trust for Scotland information board.
The 1,600 Highlanders were ranged up the hillside to the north of the road with 250 Spanish troops next to the river and Lord George Murray's men south of the river. The English mortars played on the defences close to the river, doing no considerable damage except to morale, and the afternoon saw little action until 5pm when General Joseph Wightman's right climbed round the Highlanders' left. Murray's men fell back and the Jacobites swiftly collapsed, fleeing into the hills. The Spaniards, with no such option, surrendered.

Bernera Barracks
Location: Eight miles west of Shiel Bridge via Glenelg.
Bernera is one of four barracks built in the 1720s and it survives largely as it was. The Glenelg Brochs, stone towers, are nearby.

Fort Augustus and Kiliwhimen Barracks
Location: The Benedictine Abbey and the Lovat Arms Hotel in Fort Augustus.
Kiliwhimen was the largest of the barracks built after the failure of the 1715 uprising, housing six companies (360 men). General Wade declared himself dissatisfied with it in 1724 when it was scarcely finished. He built a new fortress close to the loch, a square fort with huge corner bastions, only one of which survives at the Abbey. The barracks, too, have gone, leaving just one stretch of musket-looped wall behind the hotel.

The Military Road
The B862 to Whitebridge, along the south of Loch Ness, is a military road. A mile south of Fort Augustus, off the A82 to Fort William, is a minor road running south-east on the south-west side of Glen Tarff. This is one end of the military road over the Corrieyairack Pass, negotiable only on foot over the pass itself.

Fort William
Location: In Fort William, behind the railway station on the north of the town and at Craigs Burial Ground.
In 1689 a new fort was based on an older one, close to the River Nevis and Loch Linnhe. It was largely destroyed in 1889 to make way for the railway station. Parts of the north and west bastion, including the sallyport, are to be found behind the station and the burial ground boasts the old main gate as well as soldiers' headstones.

The West Highland Museum
Location: Cameron Square, Fort William.
Tel: (01397) 702169
Information on the fort and on the Jacobite risings.

Glencoe
Location: Seventeen miles south of Fort William by A82. National Trust for Scotland Vistor Center.
Tel: (01855) 811307 (summer only).

Glenfinnan
Location: Eighteen miles west of Fort William by A830. National Trust for Scotland Monument (open site) and Visitor Centre, open April to October daily. Tel: (01397) 722250.
Here Prince Charles Edward, the Young Pretender, raised his standard on 19 August 1745. The story of the 1745 rebellion is told in full at the Visitor Centre.

North-east Scotland

Fort George
Location: Four miles north of the A96 Inverness-Nairn road, via Ardersier. Historic Scotland. Open all year. Tel: (01667) 462777.
The original fort of this name was built on the site of Inverness Castle on which Cromwell had built a citadel. It was taken by the Jacobites in 1746 and blown up. A new fort was built some eleven miles north-east on the southern shore of the Moray Firth in 1747. The result is one of the finest, and largest, fortresses in Britain. Virtually unaltered to this day, it is a superb example of the 18th century artillery fort. Reconstructed barrack rooms portray the life of the Hanoverian soldier and the Seafield Collection of arms completes the picture.

The Battle of Culloden Moor, 16 April 1746
Location: Five miles east of Inverness by B9006. National Trust for Scotland Visitor Centre, open daily all year. Tel: (01463) 790607. Numerous landmarks and memorials also in the care of the Trust.

The Scottish line, of only 3,800 men, was formed, according to Stuart Reid, between the corner of the wall around Culloden House and the wall of the Culwhiniac enclosure to the south-east. There was no coherent second line, but a few units were in reserve. The Atholls on the right faced a turf enclosure at Leanach and they pushed left and forward to stand clear of it, pulling the line out of shape. The English had been forming in three lines with their left, Barrell's 4th Foot straddling the road in front of the Well of the Dead. The English front line was of some 3,000 men and the same number formed the second. Down the slope to the River Nairn there were some 450 English horse with infantry support who were to threaten the Jacobite rear during the battle.

At about 1 o'clock the Scots' artillery opened fire and the English replied in kind. The English aimed high to drop their cannonballs into the Jacobite lines. This fire was withstood for only ten minutes before the Highlanders on the right rushed forward. The English guns replied with canister. The Scots smashed into the English front line and were then outflanked by the second line who moved forward to contain them. Nowhere else was the English line even dented. Unsupported and almost surrounded, the Highland right fell back. The collapse spread and the English swept forward. The rout began. The battle had lasted less than an hour.

Ruthven Barracks
Location: Kingussie. Historic Scotland.

Ruthven in Badenoch was chosen as the site of one of the four barracks built in the aftermath of the 1715 uprising. Completed in 1724, it consists of two blocks facing each other across a square secured at either end with walls with musket-loops and a walkway above, enough to resist lightly armed troops but not artillery, and corner turrets to enfilade attacks. The complement was 120 men and stables for 30 Dragoons were added in 1734. The barracks were taken by the Jacobites in 1746 and their forces regrouped here after the Battle of Culloden, only to disperse in despair when the order came to fend for themselves. The buildings, now roofless, stand much as they did then.

The Military Road
Location: Laggan, eleven miles west of Kingussie by A86, and minor road straight on up the Spey valley.

In 1727 General Wade proposed a road from Loch Ness to Ruthven over the Corrieyairack Pass. It may be traced past Garvamore Barracks west of Laggan by car, but only on foot all the way to Glen Tarff and Fort Augustus.

Braemar Castle
Location: North of the A93 just east of Braemar.

A tower house where the Earl of Mar raised his standard in 1715, it was forfeit on the failure of the rising. It was leased for 99 years for a rent of £14 a year to the Hanoverian government in 1748 and converted into a barracks for occupying troops. The star-shaped outer wall was added at this time. The castle secured part of the military road, now approximating to the A93, from Blairgowrie.

Corgarff Castle
Location: Fourteen miles north of Ballater on the A939 Grantown-on-Spey road. Historic Scotland. Open daily in summer, weekends in winter. Tel (opening times): (0131) 668 8800.

The military road from Blairgowrie to Fort George, built between 1749 and 1754 and now approximating to the A93 and A939, swings up into the hills from Braemar - a route of vital strategic importance. Just to the south of the castle a length of it can be walked and north of it, on the A939, is a memorial to its builders. The 16th century tower house at Corgarff, which had been used by the Jacobites in both the '15 and the '45 rebellions, was converted to a fortified barracks by 1750.

The Battle of Killiekrankie, 27 July 1689
Location: National Trust for Scotland Visitor Centre, three miles north of Pitlochry by B8079. Open April to October. Tel: (01796) 473233. Battlesite open all year.

General Hugh Mackay had reached Urrard House by the afternoon of 27 July when Viscount Dundee's Jacobite army was coming over the high ground above the road. Their forces were hastily drawn up above the River Garry, but for two hours little took place; Mackay could not launch an attack uphill and Dundee's men had the sun in their eyes. As dusk fell the Highlanders charged the over-extended government lines and swept them away, though "Bonnie Dundee" died in the hour of victory.

Central Scotland

The Battle of Sheriffmuir, 13 November 1715
*Location: East of Dunblane (5 miles north of Stirling),
on the minor road to Blackford via Pisgah. The
Macrae Monument is where road kinks right and is
joined by path from Dunblane.*

The Earl of Mar raised his standard at Braemar on
6 September 1715. The Duke of Argyll moved the
small government force of some 3000 men to
Stirling to prevent Mar's 7000 moving into the
south of Perth. Just as the Jacobite force at
Preston was surrendering, Mar approached and
Argyll moved to meet him near Dunblane. On the
morning of 13 November 1715 the Earl of Mar
and the Duke of Argyll faced each other across
the moorland near Dunblane, about a mile and a
half apart, probably on either side of the site of
the Macrae Monument, Argyll's men with their
backs towards Dunblane. Their fronts overlapped;
Argyll's right outflanking Mar's left, and Mar's
right Argyll's left. The Scottish charge was held
and repulsed by Argyll's right while his left was
scattered and chased as far as Stirling. The battle
front turned anti-clockwise and Mar's main body
of troops were pushed back over the river at
Kinbuck to the north-west. While neither side
could claim a decisive victory on the field, the
Jacobite cause received a fatal setback.

The Battle of Falkirk, 17 January 1746
*Location: From Falkirk by B803, past junction with
B8023, bear right opposite hospital and right to
Bantaskin Park; monument and the ravine. Also,
continue past hospital on B803, stop short of sharp left
turn and look back from position of Jacobite right.*

After the failure in England, Prince Charles's
forces besieged Stirling. Lt-General Henry Hawley
brought 8,000 men from Edinburgh and Lord
George Murray answered by moving a similar
number to Falkirk Moor. Murray anchored his left
behind a ravine and formed two lines to the south
towards Glen Burn, while Hawley hurried his
troops into a line approximately through the site
of the present hospital and had his dragoons
on the left charge. They were repulsed by a
torrent of musketry and the Highlanders charged
immediately, rolling the Hanoverians back. Only
at the ravine did the line hold and the Scots found
themselves enfiladed until Murray's reserves came
up. In twenty minutes the English had been
routed but the Scots were so scattered they could

do no more than occupy Hawley's camp and
enjoy his dinner.

The Battle of Prestonpans, 21 September 1745
*Location: North of Tranent (10 miles east of
Edinburgh) on the B6371, north of the junction with
the A198.*

Sir John Cope coming from Dunbar found the
Jacobites in possession of Edinburgh and both
armies converged on Tranent. Cope deployed his
men along the present line of the railway, east of
the station, facing across the boggy land towards
the Jacobites in Tranent. Lord George Murray
declined to attack in the circumstances and
during the night led his men around to the
east, past Seton House. Cope swung his line to
form along the present B6371, but as the sun
rose the Jacobites charged. Cope's artillerymen
fled without firing a shot and the disorganised
Hanoverians had the rabid Highlanders amongst
them before they knew what was happening.

England

Carlisle Castle
*Location: Castle Way, Carlisle. English Heritage.
Tel: (01228) 591922. Open April to October daily
9.30am to 6pm, November to March 10am to 4pm.*

The castle was by-passed in the Jacobite uprising
of 1715, but had fallen into such neglect that it
was surrendered, after a short siege, to Bonnie
Prince Charlie's forces in 1745. His men soon
yielded it up, however, when the Duke of
Cumberland had cannon brought from
Whitehaven on 27 December. It is said that over
1100 shots were fired the next day and the castle
was surrendered on the 30th. An exhibition
devoted to the Jacobite risings can be seen here.
The castle also served as a prison and the graffiti
made by the unfortunates held here survive.

The Battle of Clifton Moor, 18 December 1745
Location: Clifton, two miles south of Penrith by A6.

As Lord George Murray, the Jacobite commander,
reached Clifton he learned that the Hanoverians
were close behind and observed men appearing to
the south, drawn up in two lines. They were Bland's
regiment, Kerr's Dragoons and part of Ligonier's
Horse. The Duke of Perth made for Penrith to seek
reinforcements while, in the setting sun, Murray
deployed his troops, from right to left, Glengarry

men, Col Roy Stewart's, Sterwarts of Appin and Cluny's Macphersons, about 1,000 men in all. The trap was set with the Gelgarry men concealed on the west behind a stone wall, ready to fire, Roy Stewart on the edge of the village near the church and the rest along the hedges and embankments of the lane heading south-east to Cliburn. No reinforcements arrived.

Some 500 dragoons advanced dismounted, cautiously working through the little enclosures. In the fitful moonlight they could see little, but were themselves easy to see. There was an exchange of fire with Cluny's Macphersons, followed by a charge to Murray's cry of "Claymore!" The dragoons were thrown back into the flanking fire of the Glengarry's and tried no

more. Under the cover of darkness the Jacobites withdrew safely to Penrith. The last battle on English soil had left something above two dozen dead. A monument to Bland's Regiment stands in the churchyard.

Traveller's References

Marix Evans, Martin, *The Military Heritage of Britain and Ireland*, London, André Deutsch, 1998

Seymour, William, *Battles in Britain 1066 - 1746*, Ware, Wordsworth Editions, 1997

Smurthwaite, David, *The Complete Guide to the Battlefields of Britain*, London, Michael Joseph, 1993

Tabaham, Chris and Doreen Grove, *Fortress Scotland and the Jacobites*, London, B. T. Batsford / Historic Scotland, 1996

COMPANION SERIES FROM OSPREY